Basic Tests
in
Gastroenterology

Other Examination Preparation Books Published by Petroc Press

Bateson	*MCQs in Clinical Gastroenterology*	1900603519
Bateson and Stephen	*MCQs in Gastroenterology*	1900603403
Black and Kelleher	*MCQs in Anaesthesiology*	1900603454
Chakravorty	*Visual Aids to the MRCP Examination*	0792388739
Chong and Wong	*Survival Kit for MRCP Part II*	1900603063
Edgell	*Preparing for MRCP Part II Cardiology*	0792388690
Green	*More MCQs for Finals*	079238928X
Green	*The MRCPsych Study Manual*	079238816X
Hogston	*MCQs for the MRCoG Part II*	1900603551
Kubba *et al.*	*MCQs for MFFP Part I*	1900603004
Levi	*MCQs in Psychiatry for MRCPsych*	1900603853
Levi	*PMPs for the MRCPsych Part II*	079238993X
Levi	*SAQs for the MRCPsych*	0746200994
Levy and Riordan Eva	*MCQs in Optics and Refraction*	1900603225
Levy and Riordan Eva	*MCQs for the FRCOphth*	1900603276
Levy and Riordan Eva	*MCQs for the MRCOphth*	1900603179
Mokbel	*MCQs in Neurology*	0792388577
Mokbel	*MCQs in General Surgery*	1900603101
Mokbel	*MCQs in Applied Basic Medical Sciences*	1900603756
Mokbel	*Operative Surgery and Surgical Topics for the FRCS/MRCS*	1900603705
Mokbel	*SAQs in Clinical Surgery-in-General for the FRCS*	190060390X
Ross and Emmanuel	*MCQs on Antimicrobial Therapy*	1900603411
Ross and Emmanuel	*MCQs in Medical Microbiology for MRCP*	0792388836
Ross and Emmanuel	*MCQs in Medical Microbiology and Infectious Diseases*	1900603365
Ross and Emmanuel	*MCQs in Microbiology and Infection for FRCS*	1900603152
Rymer and Higham	*Preparing for the DRCoG*	1900603012
Sanderson *et al.*	*MCQs for the MRCP Part I*	1900603802
Sandler and Sandler	*MCQs in Cardiology for MRCP Part I*	0792389999
Sandler and Sandler	*MCQs in Cardiology*	0792389387
Sandler and Sandler	*More MCQs in Cardiology for MRCP Part I*	0792388402
Sikdar	*MCQs in Basic Sciences for MRCPsych Part II*	190060356X

Obtainable from all good booksellers or, in case of difficulty, from Plymbridge Distributors Limited, Plymbridge House, Estover Road, Plymouth, Devon PL6 7PZ

Tel.   01752–202300
FAX   01752–202333

Basic Tests in Gastroenterology

by

Malcolm C. Bateson

Consultant Physician and Specialist in Gastroenterology
General Hospital, Bishop Auckland, County Durham, UK

 PETROC PRESS

Petroc Press, an imprint of LibraPharm Limited

Distributors

Plymbridge Distributors Limited, Plymbridge House, Estover Road, Plymouth PL6 7PZ, UK

Published in the United Kingdom by
LibraPharm Limited
Gemini House
162 Craven Road
NEWBURY
Berks
RG14 5NR

A catalogue record for this book is available from the British Library

ISBN 1 900603 77 2

Typeset by Martin Lister Publishing Services, Bolton-le-Sands, Carnforth, UK

Printed and bound in the United Kingdom by
MPG Books Limited, Bodmin, Cornwall PL31 1EG

Contents

Introduction

This book describes the basic tests useful in gastroenterology, and is designed to be of practical use to medical students, junior doctors in training and senior medical staff without special experience in gastroenterology.

The author has specialised in gastroenterology since 1972. He worked initially in University Hospitals in London and Dundee. From 1981 he has been a single-handed consultant in a small general hospital.

The book is based entirely on the author's own experience of the digestive diseases seen personally in modern Britain, and the tests actually available and performed. It is not exhaustively comprehensive, but aims to give a picture of what practical gastroenterology is all about.

Uncommon and downright rare diseases are important to the patients and fascinating to doctors (especially when they can demonstrate that colleagues have missed the diagnosis). However, if medical attention is mainly focused on finding the canaries it leads to an ineffective style of practice and offers a poor service to the sparrows who make up most of the workload.

The investigations are described by organ system and function groups with an appendix of diseases and appropriate investigations.

Thanks are due to many medical, laboratory and nursing colleagues, but especially to the staff of the Bishop Auckland Gastroenterology Unit, X-ray Department, Medical Photography Department, and Dr S.M. Desai.

1

Upper Digestive Endoscopy

INSTRUMENTS

For a pan-endoscopy a forward viewing instrument is usually used, with a biopsy channel which allows the obtaining of histology material. A modern standard instrument for routine use will be of about 10 mm external diameter. Smaller instruments are available for children, but the smaller the size the more floppy and difficult is the equipment to control.

Video endoscopy systems display the image on a screen so that assistants may watch too. Alternatively a teaching side-piece can be attached to fibre-optic equipment, although with some loss of illumination. The other great advantage of video equipment is improved posture for the operator. The diagnostic yields of fibre-optic and video endoscopy are identical.

PROCEDURE

It should be explained that the patient will probably be awake (but drowsy) throughout and that with sedation there may be no recollection of the procedure. It is best to provide an information sheet before the day of the procedure, and to obtain signed consent.

The stomach must be empty and this is achieved usually by fasting overnight, or by avoiding solids for at least 4 h. Clear fluids may be taken up to an hour before the test.

False teeth should be removed. Midazolam 2.5–5 mg i.v. is a useful sedative. Smaller doses of midazolam (or none at all) may be required in patients with liver decompensation or respiratory failure. Repeat doses may be required in the younger patient. In adults it is rarely useful to exceed 10 mg midazolam and paradoxical hyperactivity can occur. Heavier sedation may be needed in children, and sometimes a general anaesthetic is required. The effect of benzodiazepine sedation can be rapidly reversed if necessary by flumazenil 500 µg i.v. In patients who prefer not to be sedated, a lidocaine throat spray can be useful. It is safest not to use both sedation and throat spray. The patient lies in the left lateral position, conveniently on the trolley on which he/she will recover. A plastic gag with a central aperture to admit the endoscope is necessary to prevent the instrument being bitten. The endoscope is lubricated with water or clear jelly, and the light and suction equipment is tested before passage. The patient's head is flexed and the instrument tip is passed over the tongue to the oropharynx while an assistant holds the end with the controls. The patient is then asked to give a couple of swallows to assist passage into the oesophagus. If the patient does not comply the instrument may impact in the pharynx or enter the trachea. In either case the patient may choke and splutter, develop wheezing or coughing, and become cyanosed. If these occur the instrument should be withdrawn and a further attempt at passage made. If the trachea is entered the rough feel of the cartilages is experienced, and the branching pattern of the trachea is identified under direct vision. Guidance of the tip with a finger in the patient's mouth can be helpful. Between patients the gastroscope is sterilised by immersion for 10 min in activated glutaraldehyde.

FINDINGS

Oesophagus

A good view of the oesophagus can be obtained on entry but only usually over its lower two-thirds. Air insufflation assists vision but should be used sparingly. Macroscopic oesophagitis, Mallory–Weiss tears, stricture or carcinoma can be detected readily. *Mallory–Weiss* tears are produced by the effort of retching or vomiting. They are linear white ulcerated areas with surrounding erythema related to the level of the diaphragm. They usually occur at the gastro–oesophageal junction but in hiatus hernia are found in the cardia of the stomach. *Oesophagitis* is usually caused by retrograde reflux and extends proximally from the gastro–oesophageal junction. Mild oesophagitis is recognised by erythema, loss of surface glistening, vascular injection and friability. More severe changes lead to erosions, plaque formation and spontaneous bleeding. Discrete ulcers and benign strictures also occur, and in chronic oesophagitis the junction of the squamous and columnar epithelium can migrate proximally (Barrett's oesophagus).

Forceps passed down the biopsy channel of the instrument can obtain multiple 2–3 mm samples to provide histological proof of diagnosis. It is best to take samples for oesophagitis at least 2 cm above the gastro–oesophageal junction, since distal changes are common in healthy individuals. Samples are immediately immersed in formol saline. Cytology brushes can also be passed in the same way using a plastic catheter to protect the sample on withdrawal before immersing in fixative. It is recommended that four biopsies and cytology brushings be taken. If all are negative for carcinoma then this diagnosis is very unlikely in the oesophagus, although this is less certain for the stomach. Occasionally a tight stricture cannot be passed, but undue force must not be used. Gentle persuasion may pass the instrument through lesser strictures and give symptomatic relief. It may be possible to identify a hiatus hernia, although this is not always reliable.

The upper oesophagus and some of the pharynx can usually be seen with the narrow calibre instruments on withdrawal. Rigid oesophagoscopy by an ENT surgeon may be necessary if the post-cricoid region is under suspicion.

Stomach

On passing over the normal gastro–oesophageal junction there is a change from pale pink mucosa to the orange–red mucosa of the stomach. This does not always correlate with histological change in epithelium. It is different from the high pressure zone of the lower oesophageal sphincter, and it normally lies below the level of the diaphragm, if this can be detected.

The greater curve and the antrum are easily viewed with air insufflation if necessary, but the rest of the stomach is more difficult to examine adequately. The greater curve is recognised by its rippling longitudinal folds; the antrum is smooth. The cardia can be seen well only by putting a J-bend on the end of the instrument when it reaches the pylorus and looking back towards the oesophagus. A partial view of the lesser curve is obtained as the instrument slides over it, but again a reverse loop may be necessary to view it completely. A sharp angle or incisura may hide a small distal lesion. Often there is a pool of gastric juice on the greater curve; this may be aspirated, although care is needed to avoid damaging the mucosa. The pool can be moved by altering the patient's position slightly, or even by getting him/her to lie supine temporarily so that a full view can be obtained.

Gastritis is often distal and is recognised by loss of surface glistening, granularity, vascular injection and friability. There may be haemorrhage or superficial erosions. Some gastritis is usual after gastric surgery, in which pyloric reflux is increased. Its significance is doubtful. Also, transient erythema caused by retching is of no significance. In atrophic gastritis the stomach appears exceptionally smooth and often pale. In the auto-immune gastritis which causes pernicious anaemia, an undulating knobbly appearance is characteristic. The correlation of macroscopic gastritis and histology is very poor.

Ulcers are easily recognised; unless there has been recent bleeding they should ideally always have biopsies taken from the four quarters of the rim and from the base.

Carcinoma of the stomach can occur either as a malignant ulcer, sometimes with rolled undermined edges; or a polypoid lesion; or endoscopically normal. However, a small immobile stomach in which air is poorly retained should alert suspicion, and a mucosal biopsy may give a tissue diagnosis. A negative biopsy report never completely excludes a carcinoma, and if there is a clinical suspicion of malignancy then partial or total gastrectomy with excision biopsy should be considered in ulcer disease.

The pylorus is usually short, and of varying configuration as the peristaltic waves pass over. Ulcers can occur within the pyloric canal, and in the immediate pre- and post-pyloric regions, so that careful inspection in all stages of constriction and relaxation is rewarding. Uncommonly the pylorus is so tightly closed that the instrument cannot be passed further.

Duodenum

Duodenal ulcers typically occur in the duodenal bulb, often visible from the stomach before entering the pylorus. The duodenal folds are circumferential and the mucosa is usually paler than the stomach. The view of the duodenal bulb is adequate, but the rest of the loop is often not seen well as the instrument is advanced, and a better view is obtained during withdrawal. The ampulla of Vater may be identifiable and can be located by the jets of bile which emerge from time to time. *Duodenitis*, with erythema, oedema and friability, may occur with or without ulcers. It can be patchy so a careful examination is necessary. Biopsy confirms doubtful appearances.

Forceps biopsy of the distal duodenum is useful to find the villous atrophy of coeliac disease.

INDICATIONS

(1) Investigation of dyspepsia, of abdominal pain, and of iron deficiency anaemia.
(2) Diagnosis of haematemesis and melaena.
(3) Obtaining tissue samples for histology and cytology, especially in gastric ulcer, for microbiology in monilial oesophagitis, and in coeliac disease.
(4) Assessment of healing of gastric disease following medical treatment.
(5) Investigation of dyspepsia after gastric surgery.
(6) Evaluation of doubtful or negative barium meal appearances.
(7) Therapy:
    (a) Injection and ligation of oesophageal varices
    (b) Dilation of oesophageal strictures
    (c) Positioning of plastic and expanding metal stents
    (d) Injection and heater probe treatment of bleeding ulcers
    (e) Laser therapy, especially of oesophageal carcinoma
    (f) Positioning of nasogastric and percutaneous feeding tubes.

It is possible to introduce ultrasound (US) probes with modified (and expensive) upper digestive endoscopy equipment. It is not widely available yet and still under evaluation.

ENDOSCOPIC RETROGRADE CHOLANGIO-PANCREATOGRAPHY (ERCP) (Figures 1–3)

Instruments

Side-viewing duodenoscopes are usually used, although for difficult procedures such as in patients who have had a partial gastrectomy, forward or oblique viewing instruments may be more effective. An image intensifier and facilities for taking radiographs are both required.

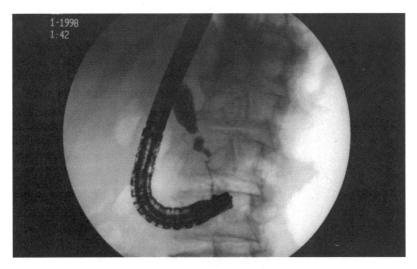

Figure 1 Endoscopic retrograde cholangiopancreatography (ERCP). Carcinoma of the pancreas with common bile duct stricture

Standard atraumatic catheters are suitable, although tapered tip catheters may be necessary for some procedures. Radiology is with 50–70% water-soluble non-ionic iodine contrast medium.

Procedure

Patients should have an i.v. cannula positioned in the right arm. If there is obstructive jaundice they should receive a 5% dextrose infusion shortly before the procedure to prevent renal failure, and a urinary catheter should be positioned. Gentamicin 80 g. i.v. is a standard prophylaxis to prevent cholangitis, and can be given an hour before or with the procedure. Blood clotting is checked: therapeutic procedures should only be performed where the haemoglobin is 10 g/dl or more, platelets $>100 \times 10^9/l$, and prothrombin time within 3 seconds of control.

Patients are positioned on the X-ray tablet semi-prone with the left arm drawn behind the left side of the body.

ERCP positioning and the procedure itself are uncomfortable and sedation with i.v. midazolam 5 mg and i.v. pethidine 50 mg is useful to assist co-operation. It is usual to give supplemental oxygen throughout the procedure.

When the stomach is reached, the duodenoscope is advanced with a slight curve on the end to identify the pylorus. The instrument is then straightened to enter the pylorus in the 'sunset' position, and when the duodenum is entered the instrument is straightened and rotated giving a view of the ampulla. The patient is then laid prone. The catheter tip is advanced into the ampulla and contrast injected with fluoroscopic screening to fill the ducts. Withdrawal and re-cannulation will usually be required to outline both

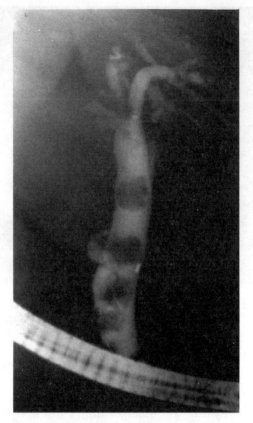

Figure 2 Endoscopic retrograde cholangiopancreatography (ERCP). Common bile duct stones

pancreatic and bile ducts. Overfilling should be avoided as it may give confusing radiographic appearances and make pancreatitis more likely.

Tilting the patient's head down will often persuade the contrast to flow into the hepatic ducts where this does not happen in the horizontal position.

When good views have been obtained, radiographs are made. It is often useful to take a further film after the duodenoscope has been removed, as it may have obscured part of the duct systems. A success rate of 90% for ERCP should be achieved with experience.

Between patients the duodenoscope is sterilised by immersion for 20 min in activated glutaraldehyde.

Indications

(1)   Confirmation of chronic pancreatitis and demonstration of pancreatic duct stones and strictures.

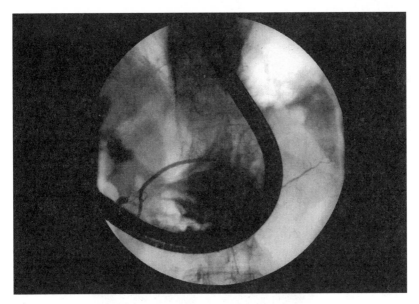

Figure 3 Endoscopic retrograde cholangiopancreatography (ERCP). Normal pancreas. Malignant stricture of common bile duct with proximal and distal dilation

(2) Diagnosis of carcinoma of the pancreas causing malignant strictures and distortion of the ducts.
(3) Obtaining pure pancreatic juice for cytology.
(4) Diagnosis of extra-hepatic cholestasis.
(5) Identification and retrieval of common bile duct stones by papillotomy and balloon or basket extraction.
(6) Identification and dilation or stenting of biliary strictures.

Relative contraindications

Recurrent acute pancreatitis and pseudocyst.

2

Oesophagus

OESOPHAGOSCOPY

Most of the disorders of the oesophagus affect the lower portion, which is conveniently inspected with a flexible pan-endoscope. If a patient has severe dysphagia, a preliminary barium swallow examination is sometimes useful. The frequent co-existence of upper digestive abnormalities means that an oesophagogastroduodenoscopy is an important investigation.

The upper oesophagus is often not well seen with the flexible endoscope, and if a thorough examination of the post-cricoid region is required rigid oesophagoscopy under general anaesthetic is best. This technique also permits the taking of larger biopsy samples.

HISTOLOGY

At endoscopy it is important to take biopsies with forceps, and also to take cytology brushings if cancer is suspected.

The usefulness of histology in benign oesophagitis is more contentious. The distal 2 cm usually has changes compatible with oesophagitis, even in normal individuals, and it is not uncommon to find changes in health above this level. The findings in oesophagitis include cellular infiltrates, increase in length of the dermal papillae and basal cell hyperplasia. Histology does not correlate well with symptoms, nor with macroscopic appearances at endoscopy. Barrett's oesophagus shows gastric and intestinal metaplasia.

RADIOLOGY (Figures 4–7)

Barium swallow

The oesophagus should be examined both during and between swallows and in the upright and lying position. The patient is frequently tilted in the head-down position to demonstrate gastro-oesophageal reflux. There are various manoeuvres to bring out diffuse oesophageal spasm, oesophageal rings and other motor disturbances of the oesophagus. The use of thick barium is one; even more informative is a 'bread bolus' in which a mouthful of bread is partially chewed and then swallowed with a mouthful of barium solution. This is useful to define length of strictures and pharyngeal pouches.

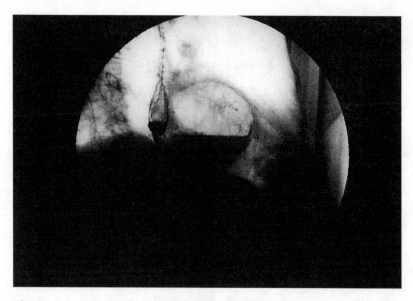

Figure 4 Barium swallow. Rolling hiatus hernia

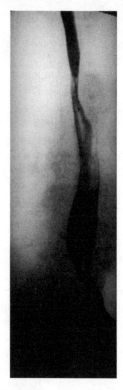

Figure 5 Barium swallow. Achalasia

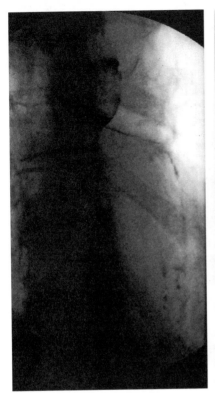

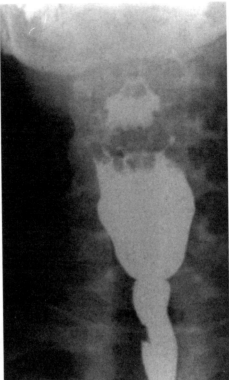

Figure 6 Barium swallow. Carcinoma   **Figure 7** Barium swallow. Oesophageal web
of the oesophagus

CT scanning is a basic test for staging oesophageal carcinoma. However, *MRI scanning* and endosonography are challengers in evaluation of extent. Both are reported to give superior results (Chapter 13, Figure 31).

MANOMETRY (Figures 8, 9)

Oesophageal motility studies are particularly valuable in the early diagnosis of achalasia of the cardia and in various motor disorders. The apparatus consists of a multi-channel pressure recorder and a series of tubes to conduct the oesophageal pressure. Scrupulous attention to detail is necessary to obtain interpretable results.

Method

Pressure recordings are taken in the stomach, at the gastro-oesophageal region and in the oesophagus both during and between swallowing. The patient can be studied while drinking 10 ml of water or during a 'dry' swallow.

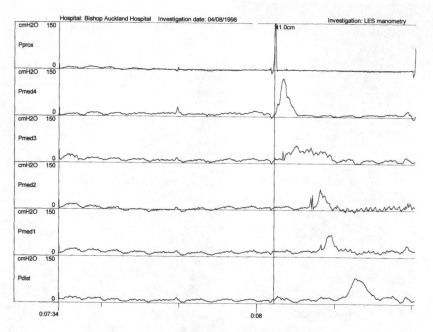

Figure 8 Oesophageal manometry. Normal swallow; pressure wave 80–200 mmH2O moves down oesophagus in orderly fashion over about 10 s

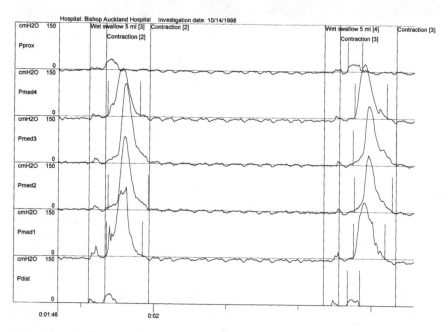

Figure 9 Oesophageal manometry. Nutcracker oesophagus – non-propagating hypertensive peaks

Recordings are made with the tube fixed at different levels throughout the oesophagus ('station' method). There is controversy over whether a rapid pull-through technique is superior; it certainly gives different results from the standard station method.

Ambulatory 24-h manometry of the oesophagus may be the most sensitive test of motility disorders.

Interpretation

Normal swallowing

On withdrawal of the tube from stomach to oesophagus there is a pressure reversal, the positive intra-abdominal pressure changing to a negative intra-thoracic pressure. The normal resting intra-oesophageal pressure is between −2 and −20 cm water.

When the patient swallows, a positive pressure wave of 40–80 cm water, which is co-ordinated and regular, sweeps down the oesophagus. A zone of increased pressure is present 2–3 cm above the gastro–oesophageal junction. This relaxes during swallowing, the relaxation preceding the arrival of the peristaltic wave.

Achalasia of the cardia

There is an absence of regular peristaltic contractions in the body of the oesophagus and there is failure of the lower oesophageal sphincter to relax during swallowing. The resting tone of the lower oesophageal sphincter is normal.

Diffuse spasm

Inco-ordinate (tertiary) contractions of the lower half to one-third of the oesophagus will be recorded and the resting pressure in the oesophagus may be raised to 200–400 cm water. The lower oesophageal sphincter functions normally although it may be included in the inco-ordinate contractions.

Scleroderma

The lower three-quarters of the oesophagus shows feeble simultaneous contractions, while the upper quarter retains normal function. There is a decline in the tone of the sphincter. At a later stage the motility disorder resembles achalasia of the cardia.

Gastro-oesophageal reflux

Sphincter tone is typically reduced.

Hiatus hernia

Four characteristic changes have been described.

(1) A double respiratory reversal point on withdrawing the recording device through the hernial sac: positive pressure in the stomach, negative in the hiatus, positive in the hernial sac and finally negative as the sphincter is passed.
(2) Two pressure peaks representing the oesophageal hiatus and the gastro-oesophageal sphincter.
(3) A plateau of positive pressure in the hernia.
(4) An increased length of the zone of high pressure.

Symptoms of oesophageal reflux are sometimes but not always associated with hiatus hernia.

REFLUX STUDIES (Figures 10, 11)

The failure of other tests to discriminate absolutely between normal subjects and patients thought to have oesophageal reflux symptoms has led to more elaborate procedures.

Method

Short-term studies

Intra-oesophageal pH is measured by an electrode or radio-pill. The probe is positioned in the stomach and then withdrawn up the oesophagus past the high-pressure zone (as defined by manometry) with continuous pH monitoring. The test is repeated after instillation of 250–300 ml 0.1 mol/l HCl in the

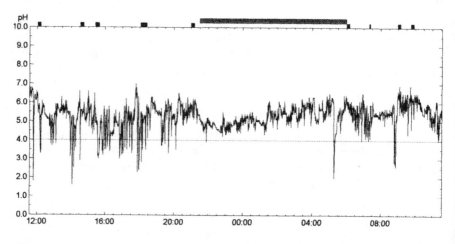

Figure 10 Twenty-four-hour oesophageal pH monitoring. Normal

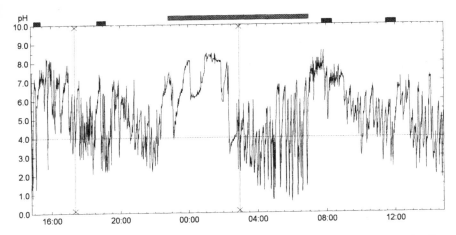

Figure 11 Twenty-four-hour oesophageal pH monitoring. Severe prolonged reflux day and night

stomach, and with both tests the level at which the pH reaches 4 is recorded. In a positive test pH falls below 4 above the high-pressure zone. A further modification is to position the pH electrode 5 cm above the high-pressure zone and perform manoeuvres such as head tilting, deep breathing, Valsalva and coughing to precipitate reflux as defined by a fall in pH of 2 units or more.

Long-term studies

The pH electrode is positioned 5 cm proximal to the high pressure zone and taped into position. Where manometry is not available the pH step locates the high-pressure zone within 3 cm. Radiographic screening before and after the test confirms that there is no displacement. Continuous monitoring is then conducted for 24 h. Any fall in pH of 2 units or more which lasts 1 minute or more is recorded as a reflux episode. The number and duration of reflux episodes is recorded. The length of time oesophageal pH is below 4 is the best discriminant and should be less than 6% time supine and 10.5% time erect in normal subjects. Ideally the total exposure to pH <4 should be less than 5% in adults, but there are many different criteria of abnormality used. In children the cut-off is much higher, at total acid exposure pH <4 of 18% or less.

ISOTOPE SWALLOW

Method

While lying under a gamma camera the fasting patient is asked to swallow a small volume of water containing 4–10 MBq of technetium-99m colloid. This is conveniently injected into the mouth by a short flexible tube connected to a 20 ml syringe. The isotope can be followed into the stomach, and normally at least 90% of the activity should have left the oesophagus in 15 s. Healthy young subjects generally clear all the activity into the stomach within 10 s. The test is repeated twice to ensure reproducibility. The test may be extended by then allowing the patient to sit up and swallow 300 ml 0.1 mol/l HCl flavoured with orange juice. Distal oesophageal scanning is then repeated with the patient supine to see if spontaneous reflux occurs from the stomach. If no spontaneous reflux is seen then external abdominal pressure can be applied with a thigh blood pressure cuff inflated to 20, 40, 60, 80 and finally 100 mmHg external pressure at half-minute intervals, with continuous oesophageal scanning.

Interpretation

Normally 10% or less of the isotope remains in the oesophagus at 15 s, and clearance is smoothly progressive. At least two out of three swallows should be abnormal before the test is regarded as positive. No reflux within the oesophagus or from the stomach should be seen.

In *achalasia* the pattern is grossly distorted with accumulation of isotope in an akinetic oesophagus.

In *oesophageal dysmotility* clearance is delayed and incomplete during the examination. There may be oscillation of bolus of isotope, indicating intra-oesophageal reflux.

In *gastro-oesophageal reflux* isotope re-enters the oesophagus from the stomach. This test is most helpful when the reflux is spontaneous rather than when it has to be induced by raising abdominal pressure artificially. In children, significant reflux is often gross, and a simple ultrasonography technique may be preferable.

Precaution

Secondary motility disorders are common, and an upper digestive endoscopy is obligatory to the interpretation of isotope swallow results. Not only may oesophageal strictures or carcinomas affect motility, but also apparently separate problems such as a duodenal ulcer can do so as well. The presence of isotope in a large hiatus hernia may masquerade either as delayed emptying or as gastro-oesophageal reflux: the pattern can be recognised for what it is with experience.

The most serious drawbacks of isotope studies are that motility disorders are common with advancing age and may not explain symptoms, and that a separate classification of disease is required from those used in endoscopy, histology and manometry.

Despite these problems isotope swallow studies are very useful since they are convenient, well-tolerated, quick and cheap.

OMEPRAZOLE TEST

In non-cardiac chest pain a useful simple clinical test is the use of a proton pump inhibitor for a week, such as omeprazole 40 mg b.d. × 7 days. If symptoms are completely abolished they may reasonably be blamed on acid reflux. This test is about 80% sensitive and 85% specific.

3
Stomach

GASTRIC ACID SECRETION

Short pentagastrin test (Peak acid output, PAO)

Method

Antacids are stopped at least a day before the test. Ideally atropinics, tricyclic antidepressants, H_2-receptor antagonists or proton pump inhibitors should be discontinued a week before the test. The patient is weighed. After an overnight fast a nasogastric tube is passed into the stomach. The patient is positioned on the left side and the aspiration ports are positioned under the surface of the pool of gastric juice. Occasionally fluoroscopy or a radiographic film are necessary to locate the tube, but in the hands of an experienced operator this is not generally required. The patient is asked to spit out saliva during the test. The stomach is aspirated and the overnight secretion is discarded.

Pentagastrin 6 µg/kg is then given subcutaneously (or intramuscularly). In the 10 min after the injection, the gastric secretion is collected either by intermittent syringe aspiration or by electric suction pump with a sub-atmospheric pressure of –5 mmHg. This collection is discarded. All the gastric secretion saved from 10–30 min after the pentagastrin injection is collected and saved. The volume and pH are measured and acidity is measured by titration against 0.01 mol/l NaOH to pH 7. The tube is removed and the whole test usually complete within 45 min.

Interpretation

There is a large individual variation in tests and a large overlap between groups with different conditions. Results will depend on patients' build: height and lean body mass are both important. For adults these are usually neglected, but in children results should be expressed as µmol/kg/h.

Normal acid secretion is usually taken to be 10–30 mmol/h for women and 15–40 mmol/h for men. Studies of endoscopy-normal dyspeptic patients and apparently healthy volunteers show that values often fall outside these ranges. Younger subjects have rather higher values, and over the age of 50 years the difference between the sexes becomes less marked. Any disease, apart from *pernicious anaemia*, may be found in the presence of normal acid secretion.

Benign gastric ulcer is in general associated with normal acid secretion. However, the more proximal the ulcer the lower the acid output; conversely, patients with pyloric and prepyloric ulcers tend to be hypersecretors.

Achlorhydria. The absence of any titratable acid in a stomach may occur in apparently normal individuals and becomes commoner with ageing. It is also found in the auto-immune gastritis of pernicious anaemia, in iron deficiency, in atrophic gastritis and some gastric cancer.

Reduced acid secretion. A peak acid output (PAO) of less than 10 mmol/h in women and less than 15 mmol/h in men virtually excludes active duodenal ulcer. This may be important where radiology shows only deformity of the duodenal cap and endoscopy does not identify an active ulcer in a patient with dyspepsia. A low acid output is characteristic of gastric cancer, but is certainly not pathognomonic and is not always associated with the condition.

Increased acid secretion is characteristically found in duodenal ulcer, though half of these patients have a normal acid output. It is occasionally caused by gastrinoma or hypercalcaemia. The hypersecretion tends to be more marked in patients with duodenal ulcer complications.

Basal acid secretion

The test should only be performed in special circumstances, e.g. when gastrinoma is suspected.

Method

The patient is intubated after an overnight fast. The overnight juice is aspirated and its volume, pH and titratable acidity are measured. The stomach is then aspirated for 1 h without any stimulation and the volume, pH and titratable acidity are measured. To ensure the most reliable results the collection should be fractionated into 4×15-min periods and the results of the analyses summated. The basal acid output (BAO) is expressed in mmol/h. Pentagastrin-stimulated PAO should then be measured to obtain the maximum useful information.

Results

In *achlorhydria* the BAO and the PAO are both nil, and the PAO is much more reliable. In duodenal ulcer the BAO is raised, as is the acidity and volume of overnight juice: the ratio of BAO/PAO is the same as in normals.

In *gastrin-induction hypersecretion*, e.g. with a gastrinoma, the BAO is at least 60% of the PAO, and the two values are usually the same. The PAO may not be markedly raised.

Intravenous technetium-99m

Another approach is the intravenous injection of technetium-99m pertechnetate 15 min after pentagastrin 6 µg/kg subcutaneously. A scintiscan over the stomach is performed 15 min later and the activity is directly proportional to acid output ($r = 0.87$). This technique may also be useful for the identification of ectopic gastric tissue in a Meckel's diverticulum.

Serum gastrin

There is a whole family of circulating gastrins but modern assays concentrate on G17. This is the 'small' gastrin with 17 amino acid residues, including one sulphated tyrosine residue. Levels rise in the circulating blood in response to a meal.

Interpretation

The normal range in fasting serum is 5–50 pmol/l (1 pmol/l is equivalent of 2.1 pg/ml). It is not raised in duodenal ulcer disease and is of no help in diagnosis unless a gastrinoma or G-cell hyperplasia is suspected because of severe, atypical or recurrent ulceration. The diagnosis then rests on a BAO/PAO ratio >60% and a fasting serum gastrin of >100 pmol/l.

Problems of interpretation

(1) The serum gastrin may be elevated without gastric hypersecretion in pernicious anaemia, hypochlorhydria, rheumatoid arthritis and in renal failure. It rises on proton pump inhibitor therapy.
(2) The serum gastrin is low when gastric surgery removes the antrum, but rises when vagotomy is performed with antral retention. Often postvagotomy values are three to four times the upper limit of normal in the absence of hypersecretion.

Vitamin B$_{12}$ urinary excretion (Schilling test)

Method

A useful test is the Dicopac method in which intrinsic-factor bound vitamin B$_{12}$ and free vitamin B$_{12}$ are given orally simultaneously. Each of the two B$_{12}$ fractions is labelled with a different isotope of cobalt, ^{57}Co and ^{58}Co respectively, and a 24-h urine collection is analysed by differential counting.

Interpretation

The results are expressed as a percentage of the dose ingested. Normally, 10% or more of the dose is excreted in the urine during the first 24 h. A low value for [58]Co suggests either an absence of intrinsic factor or defective absorption of vitamin B_{12} by the terminal ileum. It can sometimes occur in pancreatic disease because of absence of R factor. The excretion of [[57]Co]B_{12} is normal Addisonian pernicious anaemia. Low values for [58]Co are also found in the blind loop syndrome and jejunal diverticulosis, but values are usually higher (2–7%) than in Addisonian pernicious anaemia (0–3%).

A low value of excretion for [57]Co test which is similar to [58]Co suggests that the terminal ileum is diseased or absent.

Serum vitamin B_{12}

Normal results are from 200–800 pg/ml. Values are *very low* in pernicious anaemia, *low* in bacterial overgrowth of the gut and intestinal hurry, and often *high* in parenchymal or neoplastic liver disease.

Gastric antibodies

Parietal cell antibodies

About 10% of 'normal' subjects and 60–90% of patients with pernicious anaemia have circulating parietal cell antibodies. Parietal cell antibodies are never found in the presence of a normal gastric mucosa; their presence in serum or gastric juice suggests chronic gastritis and is associated with some reduction in gastric acid output. They may be present in patients with chronic gastritis who do not have pernicious anaemia. On the other hand, patients with advanced chronic gastritis may have no parietal cell antibodies.

Intrinsic factor antibodies

Antibodies to intrinsic factor are rarely found in normal sera. About 30–60% of patients with pernicious anaemia have antibodies against intrinsic factor. Large doses of vitamin B_{12} given intramuscularly within 48 h of testing the serum can cause false-positive tests for intrinsic factor antibodies.

GASTRIC CYTOLOGY

Exfoliative cytology is of great value in the diagnosis of gastric lesions, particularly cancer.

The use of the cytology brush at endoscopy combined with examination of the smears by experienced cytologists is claimed to yield better results than the histology of endoscopic biopsies. Additional material may be obtained by washing the endoscope after the examination with 200 ml physiological saline, which yields tens of thousands of cells.

Cytological interpretation is said to be easy in about 80% of gastric cancers. Gastric Hodgkin's disease and lymphosarcoma can also be diagnosed from the smears. The method is reliable and false-positive results need not exceed 0.5%. It is probably the most accurate method of establishing a pre-operative diagnosis of gastric cancer and is of particular value when deformities of the fundus or antrum are present. Failures in diagnosis are not common due to faulty interpretation, and are more probably the consequence of inadequate cell collection.

GASTRIC BIOPSY

This is conveniently performed with the endoscope biopsy forceps.

Interpretation

The *normal* stomach has variable architecture, and it is necessary to take biopsies from stated and standardised positions to enable proper interpretation. One biopsy from the antrum, two from different parts of the greater curve and one from the mid-lesser curve provide a fair sampling procedure.

Acute gastritis is characterised by infiltration of leucocytes, mucosal haemorrhages and erosions. It may be patchy so that biopsy appearances do not always correlate with endoscopy appearances.

Chronic gastritis may result from *H. pylori* infection, pyloric reflux or from gastric surgery, or other causes which may not be identifiable. Its relationship with symptoms remains doubtful. In the initial stage it is probably accompanied by gastric acid hypersecretion, but eventually hyposecretion supervenes. Whether this is cause or effect is contentious.

There is deep infiltration with mononuclear cells and glandular destruction. In severe gastritis, atrophy or metaplasia may occur, and the whole gastric mucosa may resemble the antral glandular structure or even the small intestinal architecture.

In *pernicious anaemia* a distinct pattern is seen. The stomach is involved in an auto-immune (type A) gastritis characterised by an intensely cellular atrophic mucosa containing many lymphocytes and plasma cells.

Carcinoma is usually recognised macroscopically, but carcinoma-in-situ is well recognised to occur in ostensibly normal mucosa. The epithelium may also appear normal in leather-bottle stomach, when adequate histology is diagnostic. *Cellular atypia* is sometimes reported but its significance is even less certain than such changes in the colon. The extent of gastric carcinoma may be assessed by spraying the stomach with congo red at endoscopy or operation (non-carcinomatous acid-secreting areas appear black), or by pre-treatment of patients with toluidine blue.

RADIOLOGY

Barium meal (Figures 12–14)

Gastric ulcers and benign and malignant tumours

Differentiation between benign and malignant gastric ulcer may be difficult. Some of the important features of a malignant gastric ulcer are rigid angular margins to the ulcer, a long shallow ulcer having irregular edges, an ulcer lying within the line of the gastric profile, a clear zone separating the ulcer from the barium in the stomach and the barium-filled crater, irregular translucency around the base and the disappearance of the ulcer with no lessening of the surrounding rigidity. Carcinomas may also appear as polyps or diffuse infiltration (leather bottle stomach).

Duodenal ulcer

The barium meal is sometimes important in diagnosis, but it may be very difficult to establish the presence of active ulceration in the presence of a scarred duodenal cap.

Iodinated water-soluble opaque media

The older agents (e.g. Gastrograffin) are justifiably unpopular with many radiologists. Such materials are hypertonic and are markedly diluted in the bowel to give very poor contrast. They are dangerous in the dehydrated patient, particularly infants. Newer agents such as Gastromiro are safer but much more expensive. In an emergency, where much vomiting is present and inhalation is feared, it is still better to use a dilute barium suspension than other media.

However, the water-soluble opaque agents are recommended when perforation is suspected because extravasation of these media is harmless. The new non-ionic agents are useful in dysphagia, where aspiration is a risk.

Double-contrast radiology

The introduction of the double-contrast barium meal, in which effervescent tablets or carbonated drinks are used, has improved diagnostic accuracy. Mucosal lesions can be identified much more readily, and in the hands of enthusiasts, overall accuracy can equal that of endoscopy.

Computed tomography and magnetic resonance imaging

CT and MRI are useful secondary procedures for gauging the extent and operability of gastric, and more especially of gastro-oesophageal and oeso-

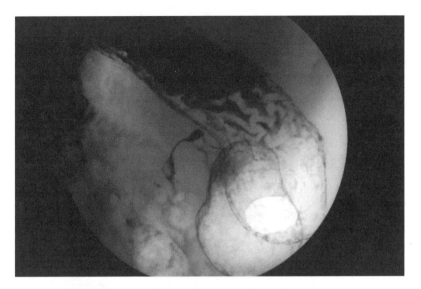

Figure 12 Barium meal. Chronic duodenal ulcer with scarring

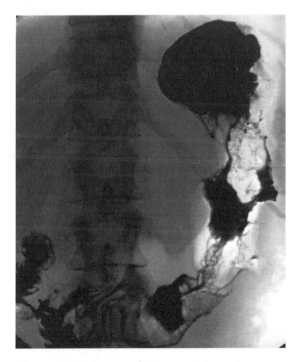

Figure 13 Barium meal. Large gastric carcinoma

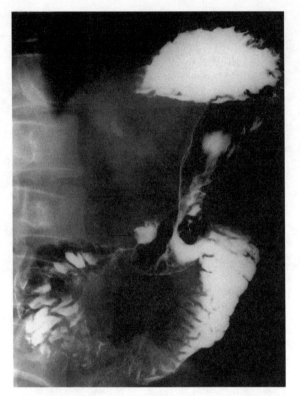

Figure 14 Barium meal. Large benign gastric ulcer

phageal carcinomas. Not only can the size and position of tumours be assessed, but also the presence of metastases in nodes, liver and lung.

Ultrasonography also has a similar role, which is especially valuable when performed endoscopically as *endosonography*.

4

Helicobacter pylori

Helicobacter pylori infection is strongly associated with age and inversely with wealth.

There appears to be an enhanced risk of infection in childhood and a lower rate in adult life.

In British provincial patients with normal gastroscopy the overall infection rate is 45%. However, this rises from 30% in late teenagers to 60% in 60-year-olds.

Helicobacter pylori is associated with duodenal ulcer disease. The figure quoted is 95% and it is probably correct to take the presence of active duodenal ulcer as an absolute indicator of current *H. pylori* infection in patients not on aspirin or non-steroidal anti-inflammatory drugs. A similar but weaker association is documented for benign gastric ulcer (75%).

There is no lymphoid tissue in normal stomach, and the presence of this, particularly if it has progressed to a mucosa-associated lymphoid tumour, is also strong evidence of *H. pylori* infection.

H. pylori infection is normally global in the stomach, but histological changes are mainly located in the gastric antrum where glandular destruction, polymorph and lymphocyte infiltration deeper than the epithelium, intestinal metaplasia, and gastric erosions are all common. Unfortunately the macroscopic recognition of gastritis caused by *H. pylori* infection is completely unreliable and histological proof is always required.

DIAGNOSTIC TESTS

Presence of active duodenal ulcer

In patients with current active duodenal ulcer disease, and who are not taking ulcerogenic drugs, it may be assumed that *H. pylori* is present and no other tests are necessary to prove the point. Although benign gastric ulcer, antral gastritis and gastric mucosa-associated lymphoid tumour (MALToma) are also linked with *H. pylori*, it is necessary to seek supporting evidence of active infection.

Direct urease test (Figure 15)

At the time of gastroscopy a biopsy can be taken and examined for urease activity.

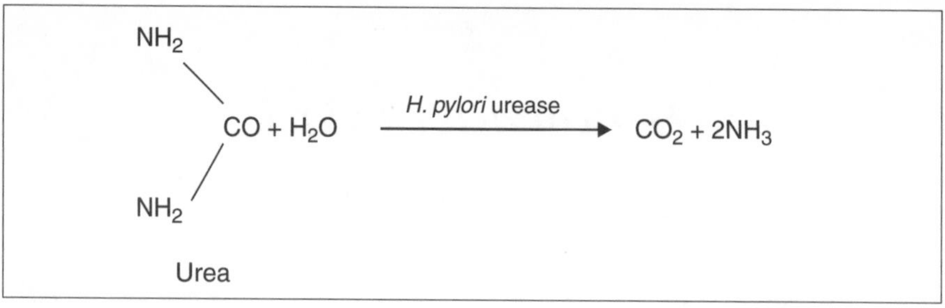

$$NH_2 \quad CO + H_2O \xrightarrow{\textit{H. pylori} \text{ urease}} CO_2 + 2NH_3$$

Urea

Figure 15 Urease activity

Almost uniquely among gastric pathogens, *H. pylori* possesses a very potent urease. When urease activity can be demonstrated in a gastric antral biopsy this is one of the best sorts for evidence of current infection.

Commercially available slides containing *urea gel* and an indicator are available, e.g. CLO-test. The antral biopsy is embedded in the gel and the end point is an indicator colour change to magenta, showing that pH has risen with the generation of ammonia. Most positive results become available within minutes, but 5–10% of true-positive results only become available in hours and it is best to read slides the next morning before discarding them. Although intrinsically very sensitive, this test may give false-negative results if patients have current upper gastrointestinal bleeding, or have recently been taking antibiotics, proton pump inhibitors or bismuth. In addition, where specific anti-Helicobacter therapy has been given there may be differential clearing in the gastric antrum so that a biopsy should be taken from the fundus or body of the stomach as well as the gastric antrum, though they may be tested on the same slide.

A cheap alternative to this system is the use of home-made *urea solution*. A solution of 0.5 ml of 10% weight/volume aqueous urea is placed in an Eppendorf centrifuge tube with a drop of phenol red and no buffer. Gastric antral biopsies are immersed in the solution. The earliest colour change is a vivid pink halo around the biopsy, although this eventually colours the whole cell to magenta. Urea solution testing was originally hoped to be more rapid than urea gel testing but this is definitely not the case and tests need to be read the following day to avoid missing some positives. Test solutions may be stored for a couple of days in a refrigerator, but are best discarded after this and a fresh batch made.

Histology

Gastric antral biopsies may be fixed in the usual way and examined under the microscope for spiral Gram negative organism with bulb-ended flagella. Most laboratories use a modified Giemsa technique. It is more controversial whether standard haematoxylin and eosin staining is as reliable. There will also be evidence of chronic gastritis when *H. pylori* infection is present.

Culture

H. pylori is a fastidious organism. Demonstration of growth requires patience and even under optimal conditions 10% of cultures may fail altogether.

Gastric antral biopsies are taken and either immediately immersed in transport medium and sent to the laboratory or plated at once.

Culture is conducted for up to 7 days on agar enriched with lyophilised horse blood in an atmosphere of reduced oxygen and 10% CO_2. Four antibiotics (vancomycin, amphotericin, cefsulodine and trimethoprim) are normally added to cultures to suppress growth of other organisms, but even so, fungal overgrowth is sometimes observed.

Cultures should be put up in parallel with a control culture of known viable *H. pylori* to ensure that technical failures are not dismissed as true negatives.

Anti-microbial sensitivity testing can only be assessed after successful microbiological culture. It is possible to use qualitative discs impregnated with antibiotics. However, a more recent quantitative technique for assessing different minimum inhibitory concentrations may be more useful. This is the E-test.

Serology

Patients who are infected with *H. pylori,* or who have been in the fairly recent past, regularly carry an IgG antibody as a marker. This can be conveniently detected using a double-antibody ELISA technique. Commercial kits are available, but comparable results can be obtained using home-made poly-valent antigen, e.g. by sonicating *H. pylori* cultures.

This is a very useful epidemiological tool for population surveys but there are difficulties when it is used in individual patients. IgG antibody may persist for 6–12 months or longer after eradication of *H. pylori,* and the change may be one of titre, rather than positive results becoming absolutely negative.

To avoid the need for sending serum to a laboratory, alternative techniques are under investigation.

Near-patient testing of whole blood samples obtained by finger pricks has been used, but results do not yield comparable sensitivity to formal laboratory serology, and this technique is not recommended.

Urea breath testing (Figure 15)

The urease activity of the total load of *H. pylori* in the stomach can be assessed by giving labelled urea by mouth and then measuring excretion of labelled CO_2 in breath.

Any hospital with access to a scintillation counter can perform the ^{14}C urea breath test.

A small amount (e.g. 0.2 MBq) of ^{14}C-labelled urea is given by mouth in water to fasting patients and breath is collected at 20 and 30 min in a CO_2-trapping agent for scintillation counting. The higher count is taken as the result to exclude false-negatives. A positive result is the excretion of 0.75% or more of the total radioactivity dose per millimol $CO_2 \times$ body weight in kilograms.

A ^{13}C-labelled urea breath test is similarly available, but requires a mass spectrometer. Commercial services are available via post to overcome difficulty of availability of equipment and all that is required are duplicate samples of exhaled breath 30 min after ingestion of the test dose.

Alternative techniques of detecting *H. pylori* antibodies in saliva or *H. pylori* specific antigen in stool are not generally used.

PRACTICAL USE

Where patients are attending for gastroscopy, gastric biopsy with urease testing is a convenient, cheap and rapid way of assessing the presence of *H. pylori*. Where it is required to check eradication of *H. pylori* after treatment, and to check that gastroscopy is not required, the urea breath test comes into its own. It is very important to wait at least a month after all proton pump inhibitor, antibiotic and bismuth therapy has been completed or else false-negative results may be obtained because of suppression rather than eradication of the organism.

Culture is important in order to test local antibiotic sensitivity patterns, but may not be important for individual patients.

5

Absorption

Major causes of persistent steatorrhoea are coeliac disease, chronic pancreatic disease including cystic fibrosis and pancreatic carcinoma, and gastric surgery. There are many other causes, and acute self-limiting steatorrhoea is a common feature of infective gastroenteritis and acute pancreatitis.

FATS AND RELATED SUBSTANCES

Triolein breath test (Figure 16)

Because of the practical problems of faecal fat estimation, various isotope tests have been proposed. The most satisfactory test is the triolein breath test. Glyceryl-^{14}C-triolein is given with a carrier meal and breath $^{14}CO_2$ activity is counted. Each of the three oleic acid molecules is labelled with ^{14}C. The basis of the test is that the oleic acid is absorbed after digestion of triglyceride, and metabolised in the body to $^{14}CO_2$ and H_2O.

Method

The patient is studied while eating a normal diet and while avoiding drugs which affect intestinal mobility.

After an overnight fast 0.2 MBq glyceryl-^{14}C-triolein is given by mouth with a standard 20 g liquid fat meal. Breath is collected before the test meal and hourly for 6 h afterwards. Patients are asked to exhale through a rubber tube connected to a Pasteur pipette, the end of which is under the surface of the trapping solution. This contains 2 mmol of a quarternary amine (hyamine hydroxide) in ethanol with thymolphthalein as indicator. The patients continue bubbling their exhaled gas through until the indicator turns from blue to colourless, when 2 mmol CO_2 has been trapped. $^{14}CO_2$ is then measured in each of the samples by liquid scintillation counting, and the output of $^{14}CO_2$ expressed as a percentage dose excreted per hour.

Interpretation

Normal peak excretion is greater than 0.38% dose/mmol/CO_2 body weight in kilograms.

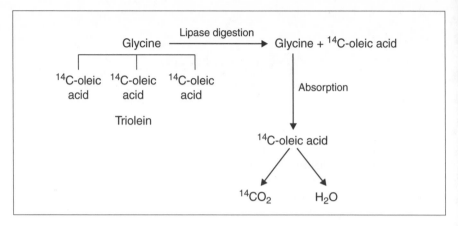

Figure 16 Triolein breath test

Indications

This test is useful when it is necessary to monitor steatorrhoea in a patient. It has been recommended as a preliminary screening test to reduce the number of faecal fat estimations.

A modification using ^{13}C-triolein and measuring breath $^{13}CO_2$ by mass spectroscopy is available to avoid the use of radioisotope.

Faecal fat excretion

Fat is present in the faeces in three forms: as neutral fat (triglycerides, 'unsplit' fat); free fatty acids ('split' fat); and sodium, potassium and calcium salts of the fatty acids (soaps). The origin of the faecal fat is not fully understood. It is in part exogenous, being derived from unabsorbed dietary fat, but also partly endogenous from the bile, desquamated cells and the breakdown of bacteria.

Method

It is important that the patient is eating a normal diet; patients with steator-rhoea often control diarrhoea by reducing fat intake. Patients should be told that satisfactory results depend on diet, and it is worthwhile arranging a consultation with the dietitian to ensure an adequate intake.

The faeces excreted over a period of 3 or 5 consecutive days are collected and sent to the laboratory. The samples should be in clearly labelled and dated containers. If the patient is constipated a longer period of collection may be required. Periods of collection shorter than 3 days are unsatisfactory and inaccurate, as the amount of fat contained in a single stool specimen can vary widely.

Plastic, radio-opaque pellets, or dye markers can be used to ensure complete collection for a given number of days. The faeces should be uncontaminated by barium and the patient must not be taking purgatives.

The collection of stools should present no problems *in hospital* where the stools passed into bedpans can be transferred to containers. The *out-patient* collection of stools is much more difficult and uncertain. The following technique has been suggested for out-patients. A polythene sheet is cut into the shape of a wide-mouthed cone 24 inches in diameter. This can be held conveniently in place between the seat and the basin of the lavatory, and after defecation the sheet and faeces are transferred to a container. One can is used for each day and at the end of the day the lid is sealed with adhesive tape. It is desirable but not essential that the cans are stored in a refrigerator until analysis.

In the laboratory the stool is mixed with water, homogenised, and the collection pooled. After thorough mixing, a 10 ml aliquot is analysed by hydrolysis, extraction and titration of the fatty acids. The result may be expressed as fatty acids but is usually expressed as amount of neutral fat excreted per day.

Interpretation

The normal maximum daily output of fat is 18 mmol or about 7 g in adults, but the upper limits vary in different laboratories. A patient who excretes more than the normal daily amount of fat in the stool is said to have steatorrhoea. There is very little difference in the amount of fat excreted in the stool when normal subjects take diets varying between 50 and 250 g fat/day but in patients with malabsorption the stool fat content is more closely related to the dietary fat intake. The ordinary mixed diet in the United Kingdom contains 70–90 g fat/day.

No markers are required in this test. The method gives poor recovery of short- and medium-chain fatty-acid triglycerides. This is normally not a problem as the average diet contains almost exclusively the long-chain triglycerides, but some artificial diets contain fat as medium-chain triglycerides which do not require digestion prior to absorption. Markers such as cuprous thiocyanate, carmine or radio-opaque pellets have been used to ensure complete collections. In theory this is an attractive method but it is handicapped by the fact that luminal contents are not homogenous and that solids, oils and aqueous solutes travel at different rates.

Indications

The faecal fat output is a widely used index of the state of digestion and absorption in the small intestine. Steatorrhoea is a feature of a number of diseases involving the small intestine, the pancreas, the hepatobiliary system, and also in many patients who have had a partial gastrectomy or vagotomy and drainage procedure. The terms steatorrhoea and malabsorption are frequently used interchangeably. Steatorrhoea implies only an excess of fat in the stool, but the presence of steatorrhoea is usually one of the cardinal features of malabsorption in which fluid, electrolytes, vitamins, carbohydrates and proteins may be poorly absorbed.

Macroscopic appearance

The macroscopic appearance of a stool containing excess fat is sometimes characteristic: bulky, yellow or grey, soft and sticky with a rancid odour. The stool may be liquid, frothy and have floating oil droplets. On the other hand, the stool may appear perfectly normal or even rather small and hard. Stools float in water because of increased gas content, which does not correlate with fat content.

Stool weight

The stool weight in Britain is normally up to a limit of 250 g/day. Steatorrhoea is unlikely but not impossible if the stool weight is less than 80 g/day. A clinically useful guide to the severity of steatorrhoea is obtained by weighing the stool daily, even though the correlation between the stool fat content and the stool weight is not close. By following progress in this way it is possible to avoid overburdening the laboratory with frequent requests for faecal fat estimation.

Prothrombin time (or International Normalised Ratio – INR)

This test reflects vitamin K absorption as well as liver synthesis. If the prothrombin time is more than 3 seconds longer than control, and reverts to normal after treatment for 3 days with vitamin K 10 mg i.m. or i.v. daily, then vitamin K malabsorption is established. This may accompany any cause of steatorrhoea. An INR of 1.3 or more gives equivalent information.

Serum vitamin D (25-hydroxy vitamin D)

In addition to dietary sources of vitamin D, there is an appreciable synthesis in the skin under the influence of daylight. Low values may be found in inadequate vitamin D intake and in individuals (especially with pigmented skins) who are not exposed to sufficient daylight. Values are markedly seasonal with higher values in summer.

The normal adult range of values is 25–75 nmol/l in summer and 15–60 nmol/l in winter. Laboratories can separate 25-OH-ergocalciferol (dietary origin), which is low in malabsorption, from 25-OH-cholecalciferol (endogenous synthesis).

Bile acid malabsorption

Some uncommon forms of diarrhoea are caused by excessive loss of bile acids into the colon from the small intestine. This can be measured by giving Selenium-75-labelled tauro-homocholic acid (^{75}SeHCAT) by mouth, and measuring retention in the body. Normal conservation of bile acids in the enterohepatic circulation means that at 24 h 80% of activity is retained in the body, 50% at 72 h, and 15% or more at 7 days. A convenient test is to count the patient's whole body with a gamma camera at 1 week to separate pathologically low retention from normal.

Although theoretically attractive this test confers no definite advantage over a therapeutic trial of bile-acid binding resin such as cholestyramine or colestipol.

Oral glucose tolerance test

This has limited application, and should not be used in patients known to be diabetic. Plasma glucose levels must be taken at defined intervals in relation to meals, and the patient must have been eating a normal diet during the 3 days before the test.

Method

Fasting blood is taken into an oxalate bottle for blood glucose estimation and a further sample is taken 2 h after a normal breakfast.

By the definition of the World Health Organization, if the fasting plasma glucose is greater than 7 mmol/l, or the postprandial plasma glucose is greater than 11 mmol/l, the patient has diabetes mellitus and no further test is useful. If not then a formal glucose tolerance test may be useful, and should be performed on a separate day as follows:

(1) A fasting blood sample is taken;
(2) The patient quickly drinks 75 g glucose dissolved in 250 ml water;
(3) Blood glucose is sampled every 30 min for 2 h;
(4) Urine is tested for sugar as often as conveniently possible.

The American Diabetes Association has recently defined diabetes as a fasting plasma glucose >7 mmol/l, and now describes four types of diabetes. Whether this is useful for gastroenterology remains to be seen.

Interpretation

A fasting plasma glucose >7 mmol/l or a plasma glucose >11 mmol/l 2 h after glucose ingestion indicates diabetes mellitus. Glycosuria supports this but is often absent in the elderly. Diabetes mellitus develops in 15% of patients with acute pancreatitis, in 70% with chronic pancreatitis (almost always when there is steatorrhoea), and in 30% with pancreatic cancer.

When there is small bowel disease causing malabsorption there is a flattened curve in non-diabetic patients, and the blood glucose does not rise more than 2 mmol/l over fasting values. However, this can also be seen in normal subjects and where gastric emptying is slow.

Where gastric emptying is rapid, as after gastric surgery, the first blood glucose level will be high, 'alimentary hyperglycaemia', followed by very low levels which may produce symptoms. This occurs because of an inappropriately timed release of insulin. If this is suspected it is best to measure blood glucose every 10–15 min after the glucose load.

DISACCHARIDES

The main disaccharidases in man are lactase, sucrase and maltase. Deficiency syndromes involving one or more of these disaccharidases have been described. Two forms of deficiency syndromes are recognised; a primary variety in which an isolated enzyme deficiency exists in an otherwise normal mucosa, and a secondary variety in which the disaccharide deficiency is only one of many enzymes which is lacking in a mucous membrane damaged from recognisable causes. By far the most common syndrome is one involving isolated lactase deficiency; this is frequent in Mediterranean and tropical countries but less common in northern Europe. It is more often seen in Negroes than Caucasians. Maltase and sucrase deficiencies are usually found in association with lactase deficiency, but infrequently occur in isolation and are then generally in children.

Lactose tolerance test

After an overnight fast the patient ingests 50 g lactose in 500 ml water. Venous blood samples are tested for glucose in the fasting state and every 30 min for 2 h.

A normal result is a rise in blood glucose of at least 1 mmol/l. A rise of less than this is considered to represent a flat absorption curve and is suggestive of lactase deficiency. Patients with normal lactase absorption curves usually have normal mucosal lactase activities. Lactose may be given in a dose of 1.5 g/kg body weight or, in children, as a dose of 50 g/m^2 of body surface. This test may also be performed using maltose or sucrose instead of lactose.

A tolerance test using 25 g glucose and 25 g galactose (the hydrolytic products of lactose) may be undertaken to confirm a diagnosis of lactase deficiency. Patients with lactase deficiency have a normal rise of blood glucose levels, and are symptom-free after ingesting the mixture of glucose and galactose, in contrast to the effects of a lactose load.

Symptomatology

Patients who have significant lactase deficiency will often develop abdominal cramps, distention, flatulence and diarrhoea 1–6 h after ingestion of 50 g lactose. At such time the stools may contain both lactic and acetic acids which result in a low stool pH of below 4 (normal pH is 7). However, an acid stool is not invariably present, particularly in adults. While the development of symptoms after 50 g lactose suggests lactase deficiency, the failure to react does not exclude intestinal lactase deficiency but implies only that the clinical syndrome is absent. Fifty grams is the approximate lactose content of a litre of milk and this volume can be used as test dose, instead of the refined sugar.

Hydrogen breath test

It has been shown that patients with disaccharidase deficiency excrete more hydrogen and less CO_2 after an appropriate disaccharide load.

In the first 3 h after 12 g lactose by mouth, patients with lactase deficiency excrete more than 20 ppm of hydrogen in the breath, whereas healthy individuals excrete less than 4 ppm.

HAEMATINICS

Vitamin B_{12}

Serum B_{12} levels are low in many diseases causing malabsorption, often because of intestinal hurry. This is non-specific. However, low serum B_{12} is commonly due to other causes such as pernicious anaemia. A Dicopac Schilling test can demonstrate the inability of the terminal ileum to absorb B_{12}-intrinsic factor complexes; it is, therefore, a useful test of terminal ileal function.

Folic acid absorption

Folic acid is absorbed in the jejunum. In addition to dietary sources folic acid may be synthesised by intestinal bacteria, and in this way elevated serum levels can occur. Red cell folate levels are more reliable than serum folate.

Iron

Iron is normally absorbed from the duodenum, or from the first normal part of the small bowel which food enters after leaving the stomach. Iron deficiency is a common feature of many disorders of absorption of the small intestine, but also occurs frequently from deficient intake and blood loss. The blood film shows hypochromia and microcytosis, i.e. pale small red cells. The serum iron is low and iron-binding capacity is raised so that percentage saturation is below 15%. Serum ferritin levels correlate fairly well with body iron stores, and in iron deficiency are below 17 µg/l.

6

Small Intestine

The function of the small bowel can be evaluated by clinical tests of absorption. Intestinal biopsy, bacteriology, radiology, radioisotope studies, enteroscopy and serology provide additional information to enable specific diagnoses to be made.

INTESTINAL BIOPSY

Endoscopic forceps biopsy is the standard procedure since it is rapid and reliable. The best results are obtained by taking multiple biopsies of the distal duodenum with the largest available size of forceps. The duodenal bulb is not ideal for non-targeted biopsy of apparently normal mucosa, but histology confirmation of visible abnormalities may occasionally be required. The widest available channel endoscope should be used with the largest compatible forceps.

Interpretation

Dissecting microscope

Normal appearance. The jejunal villi are long and finger-like and the vascular arcades are easily recognised. The height of a villus is about three times its width. Essentially similar features are found in the ileum. A normal variant is the broad, flat or leaf-shaped villus and this is seen particularly in duodenal biopsies where the leaves may even coalesce into ridges. An identical appearance may be seen in jejunal biopsy samples from normal subjects of Middle or Far Eastern extraction. These features may be identified with a hand lens.

Abnormalities. In coeliac disease the mucosal biopsy will be 'flat' or 'convoluted'. A 'flat' mucosa shows a complete loss of villi and the normal vascular arcades. There may be a mosaic or crazy pavement appearance. The 'convoluted' mucosa has no true villi but only ridges and whorls. While examination under the dissecting microscope or hand lens is a rapid and convenient diagnostic procedure it does not replace conventional histology. It is usually easy to recognise an abnormal villous pattern; the difficulty lies in deciding when villi are minimally abnormal. In this situation light microscopy is essential.

Light microscope

Normal appearance. Tall thin villi are seen lined by columnar epithelium. There are numerous goblet cells. Paneth and argentaffin cells may be seen at the base of the crypts of Lieberkühn. Mononuclear cells, plasma cells and eosinophils are seen in the lamina propria which is about one-half to one-third as thick as the villous height. Similar features are found in both finger- and leaf-shaped villi.

Brunner's glands are seen in the duodenum occupying the full thickness of the glandular (non-villous) mucosa. Villi may be blunted or absent. In the ileum more goblet cells are found, and the villi are slightly broader and shorter. There are collections of lymphoid cells, and villi overlying such areas are either stubby or absent. Specimens from apparently normal subjects in the Middle and Far East show a greater percentage of blunt and broad villi, more abnormal surface cells and slightly more prominent mononuclear cellular infiltration.

It is important to appreciate the variations in the appearance of the normal small bowel biopsy. The suggestion has been made that the 'finding of four adjacent normal villi *in any section* justifies an interpretation of normal villous architecture'.

Abnormalities

A number of diseases may be associated with minor non-specific abnormalities of the intestinal mucosa.

Coeliac disease. This is defined as the presence of total or subtotal villous atrophy which reverts to normal, or at least shows improvement, after the patient adheres to a gluten-free diet. It is important that milder abnormalities (partial villous atrophy) are not diagnosed as coeliac disease, because they are common and non-specific findings.

Children with coeliac disease characteristically have total villous atrophy. There is virtual absence of the villi, thickening of the lamina propria, increased infiltration by lymphocytes and plasma cell, elongated crypts of Lieberkühn, increase in the mucosal glands and obvious surface epithelial abnormalities with increased intra-epithelial lymphocytes. In less severe villous atrophy the villi are short, thickened and disorganised, the goblet cells are increased in number and there are lesser changes in the lamina propria. The mucosal changes in coeliac disease are seen maximally in the duodenum and upper jejunum, but in severe involvement the changes will extend to the ileum. There is no correlation between the histological abnormalities and the absorptive function. A flat biopsy is found in some patients who do not respond to gluten withdrawal, and it is not possible to predict the response from the appearance of the intestinal biopsy. The typical appearance of coeliac disease may be found in the biopsies of patients who have, or will subsequently develop, intra-abdominal lymphomas or other cancers of the gastro-intestinal tract.

Similar appearances can occur in dermatitis herpetiformis, and these sometimes respond to gluten exclusion. Psoriasis may occasionally be associated with villous atrophy.

Whipple's disease. The lamina propria is virtually replaced by macrophages filled with periodic acid–Schiff-positive glycoprotein granules. The normal villous architecture is distorted, and the lymphatics are dilated and filled with fat. Tiny bacilli can be seen with high-resolution light microscopy or with electron microscopy.

Other diseases. In the conditions described above, jejunal biopsy is invariably helpful. In some others, such as lymphangiectasia, lymphoma, giardiasis, amyloidosis and Crohn's disease, biopsy may be helpful but is not necessarily so.

Non-specific changes include mild flattening and broad thickening of the villi, an increase in chronic cellular infiltration and minimal thickening of the glandular epithelium. Such an alteration is to be found in association with hepatitis, Crohn's disease, jejunal diverticulosis, ulcerative colitis, kwashiorkor, pernicious anaemia, after partial gastrectomy and after neomycin therapy. Similar changes may be found in coeliac disease and cannot be used to substantiate the diagnosis. The mucosal biopsies are normal in disaccharide deficiency, iron deficiency anaemia, peptic ulcer disease and pancreatic disease. Villous abnormalities have been described in association with certain skin diseases such as eczema and psoriasis. These are usually minor, but occasionally a severe atrophy is present which is indistinguishable from coeliac disease.

RADIOLOGY (Figures 17, 18)

The small intestine can be studied after radiological examination of the stomach has been completed. During the course of a *small bowel meal* there may be unpredictable emptying of the stomach with irregular and excessive filling of the intestine, and the barium-filled stomach may obscure parts of the intestine. These difficulties are obviated by the use of the Scott–Harden tube which enables the duodenum to be filled rapidly by a known volume of barium. In this manner a *small bowel enema* is performed using large volumes of relatively dilute barium. It is controversial whether the small bowel meal or enema is better.

The normal small intestinal mucosa demonstrates a feathery pattern. On a follow-through in coeliac disease there is slowing of the transit time, the bowel lumen is dilated, intestinal folds appear thickened, and there is 'stacking' and clumping of the barium. Barium sulphate tends to flocculate in the presence of steatorrhoea, whether this is the consequence of intestinal or hepatic or pancreatic disease. The use of non-flocculating barium suspensions enables the radiologist to study the intestinal mucosa in the presence of steatorrhoea and it is of help in the diagnosis of Crohn's disease, strictures, diverticula and blind loops. The terminal ileum may be better outlined by retrograde barium enema than by small bowel series.

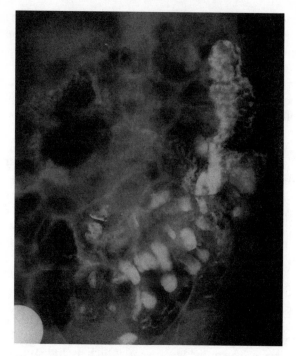

Figure 17 Small bowel meal. Diverticulosis (with bacterial overgrowth and malabsorption)

Angiography techniques are available and there is a selective technique in which the catheter is introduced into either the coeliac, or superior or inferior mesenteric artery. It is possible to demonstrate vascular lesions involving the major vessels supplying the gastrointestinal tract. In this way it is possible to demonstrate neoplastic disease of the bowel as well as the site of gastrointestinal bleeding.

Lymphangiography has proved of value in the diagnosis of retroperitoneal lesions and in the demonstration of abnormal intestinal lymphatics such as are found in intestinal lymphangiectasia.

RADIOISOTOPE STUDIES

White blood cell scanning

The patient's own white blood cells are labelled with ^{99m}Tc-HMPAO (hexamethyl propylene-amine oxime) and re-injected. Abdominal scanning will localise areas of inflammation by increased uptake. This is particularly useful in identifying sites of Crohn's disease involvement in the small and large bowel.

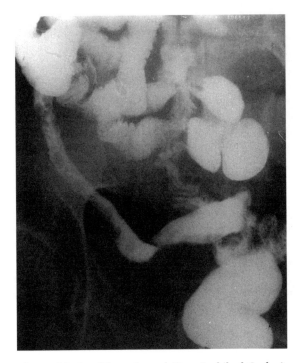

Figure 18 Small bowel meal. Terminal ileal Crohn's disease

Appearances are not specific and corroborative evidence is necessary before a complete diagnosis is made.

ENTEROSCOPY

This endoscopic examination can be performed with a dedicated instrument or a paediatric colonoscope. Usually only the jejunum is seen. This technique will provide visual information and also the possibility of biopsy in the small bowel. Conditions which can be identified are diaphragm disease and ulceration in patients on NSAIDs, angiodysplasia, tumours and Crohn's disease.

INTESTINAL BACTERIA

Under normal conditions the small bowel contains only low concentrations of micro-organisms. Bacterial overgrowth occurs in a number of disease states and the assessment of intestinal bacteria is of great value. Methods for determining the extent of bacterial proliferation in the bowel are:

(1) Culture after intubation and aspiration of small bowel contents;
(2) Biopsy of intestinal mucosa;

(3) ^{14}C-labelled glycocholate test;
(4)   Breath hydrogen assay.

Intubation

The small bowel bacterial flora can be directly identified and quantitated by intubation techniques. Intestinal bacteria may be obtained at operation by needle aspiration of the bowel, or using a simple sterilised disposable double-lumen radio-opaque tube.

Method

The intestine is intubated after an overnight fast. The patient, who must not be taking antibiotic therapy, has an alkaline gargle before swallowing the tube. The tube is screened into the desired position, aspirates being taken from the mid-jejunum or any known diseased area. The tube is withdrawn once samples have been obtained. The aspirated samples are delivered to the laboratory as rapidly as possible and plated for aerobic and anaerobic culture. A quantitative and qualitative determination is made of the bacterial population. Strict attention to culture conditions is necessary for demonstration of obligatory anaerobes. Simultaneous culture of saliva is advisable to identify non-significant contaminants.

Interpretation

Normally the jejunum is sterile, or bacterial counts are less than 10^3–10^5 per ml, the organisms being mainly of the oropharyngeal type. Counts of more than 10^5 organisms per ml indicate bacterial overgrowth, the organisms being mainly strains of *Escherichia coli* and *Bacteroides*.

^{14}C-glycocholic acid breath test (Figure 19)

This test is based on the ability of many, but not all, intestinal bacteria to deconjugate bile acids. This normally only occurs to any extent in the colon. If there is colonisation of the upper small bowel deconjugation results in the absorption of ^{14}C-labelled glycine. This is completely metabolised, producing $^{14}CO_2$ which is measured in the breath.

Method

The patient is fasted overnight. 0.2 MBq of ^{14}C-glycine-glycocholic acid is given by mouth and the patient is then allowed to eat normally. Before, and at hourly intervals for 6 h after the isotope has been administered, breath is collected by bubbling through a solution containing 1 mmol hyamine hydroxide with thymolphthalein indicator until the blue colour disappears.

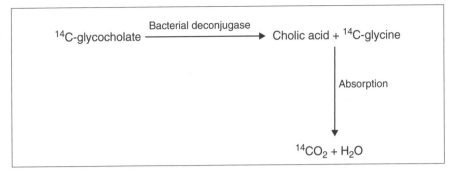

Figure 19 ^{14}C-glycocholate breath test

The radioactivity in each sample is measured by liquid scintillation counting.

Interpretation

Results are expressed as a percentage dose of ^{14}C excreted/nmol CO_2 trapped, corrected for body weight. In normal subjects values in each of the first 3 h are below 0.1%, and no value throughout the test exceeds 0.3%.

In upper small bowel bacterial overgrowth values from 2 h onwards are raised, with maximal values at 3–5 h. In cholangitis peak values are seen at 1–2 h. In intestinal hurry normal colonic bacteria may give late positive results. An internal bile fistula usually invalidates the test.

Unfortunately, this test has not fulfilled its early promise of replacing the need for small bowel intubation and direct culture.

Breath hydrogen

Bacterial colonisation of the small intestine leads to an increase in breath hydrogen to more than 20 ppm after a 50 g glucose load by mouth. Unfortunately the values may be spuriously raised in cigarette smokers, after dietary carbohydrate intake and in intestinal hurry and irritable bowel syndrome; they may be reduced by exercise and hyperventilation. The test requires very careful standardisation to be useful, despite the deceptive ease with which breath hydrogen can be monitored by automatic machines.

Breath hydrogen after 20 ml oral lactulose is a measure of orocaecal transit time.

Biopsy

Endoscopic forceps biopsy and simultaneous intestinal aspiration followed by microscopy and culture can be very helpful in diagnosis of *giardiasis.*

CROHN'S DISEASE

This is often difficult to diagnose and a number of helpful tests are available.

Excision biopsy of involved sites

Full thickness inflammation, deep ulcers and granulomas are diagnostic features. Local lymph nodes may also contain granulomas.

Barium radiology

Internal fistulas between loops of small bowel and skip lesions (diseased areas separated by normal bowel) are the most helpful findings, although a host of other abnormalities occur.

Rectal biopsies and upper gastrointestinal biopsies

Sometimes diagnostic features are seen, but often non-specific changes can be identified which support a diagnosis of organic disease.

Skin testing with tuberculin (Mantoux test), dinitrochlorbenzene (DNCB) and the Kveim test

The Mantoux test is negative in most patients with active Crohn's disease, even if they have been immunised against tuberculosis. Anergy to DNCB (i.e. no reaction after skin injection) occurs in 70% compared with 9% of controls. The Kveim test is a cutaneous injection of a prepared extract of spleen from diseased patients which provokes a granulomatous reaction, identified by histology at 6 weeks. It is positive in about half the patients with Crohn's disease.

Other tests

Colonoscopy may be able to visualise directly the terminal ileum or involved large bowel. The SeHCAT and Dicopac Schilling tests are abnormal in terminal ileitis.

Faecal fat excretion is often increased. White blood cell scanning may locate diseased areas (both active Crohn's disease and abscesses). Ultrasonography can be helpful in diagnosis. T- and B-lymphocyte functions are usually depressed, but this is variable. Laparoscopy or laparotomy is sometimes required in refractory ileo-caecal disease to exclude carcinoma, which may sometimes stimulate Crohn's disease.

Investigations for monitoring progress

Because of the variability and chronicity of Crohn's disease, attempts have been made to establish investigations which might correlate with disease

Table 1 Crohn's disease activity index

General well-being (0 = very well, 4 = terrible)

Abdominal pain (0 = rare, 3 = severe)

Daily number of liquid stools

Abdominal mass (0 = absent, 3 = definite + tender)

Complications, e.g. arthralgia, aphthous ulcers (score 1 each)

A patient who is perfectly well scores 0, and a patient who is in severe relapse scores more than 10

activity. Serial measurements of serum seromucoids and lysozyme, C-reactive protein, plasma viscosity, ESR and regular barium radiology have not proved very useful in practice.

A simple index of Crohn's disease (CDAI) activity based on history and physical examination has been found satisfactory. A similar one has been described for ulcerative colitis where evaluation is less of a problem (Chapter 7).

In addition, serial ultrasonography, serial white blood cell scanning and serial weighing in patients not on steroids, give some helpful objective data. A full blood count including platelets (raised in active disease) is a practical simple objective yardstick.

METABOLIC DISORDERS

Gastrointestinal symptoms such as pain, diarrhoea and constipation may be the most prominent features of certain metabolic disorders. During the investigation of a patient with abdominal pain, it may be helpful to determine the serum calcium (elevated in hyperparathyroidism) and to note whether the serum is lactescent (in certain forms of hyperlipidaemia). Abdominal pain may be an early feature of diabetic ketosis and a manifestation of a haemolytic crisis as in sickle cell anaemia. Hypothyroidism may present with constipation, and diarrhoea can be prominent in pellagra.

CARCINOID SYNDROME

Patients with metastases from a primary carcinoid tumour in the gut may present with a syndrome of intermittent diarrhoea, flushing, asthma and a pellagrinous rash. Occasionally diarrhoea dominates the clinical picture. Diagnostic tests are based on the knowledge that these tumours contain a high concentration of 5-hydroxytryptamine (5-HT, serotonin) which is converted to 5-hydroxyindoleacetic acid (5-HIAA) and excreted in excess in the urine. This is usually measured in a 24-h collection, but this may need to be repeated as high levels can be intermittent.

Twenty-four-hour urinary excretion

The urine is collected into a bottle containing 25 ml glacial acetic acid to preserve the 5-HIAA, which is measured in the laboratory. Normally less than 9 mg 5-HIAA are excreted in 24 h. In the carcinoid syndrome values are 40–873 mg/24 h. A moderate increase of urinary 5-HIAA (9–20 mg/24 h) has been reported in untreated adult coeliac disease, tropical sprue and Whipple's disease.

PHAEOCHROMOCYTOMA

Occasionally the possibility is raised that diarrhoea is due to the presence of a phaeochromocytoma. Diagnosis of this tumour is based on measurement of the 24-h excretion of urinary catecholamines and metabolites, which are elevated in phaeochromocytoma. The excretion of these substances is occasionally paroxysmal.

The 24-h urinary output is collected into a bottle containing 12 ml concentrated hydrochloric acid. Normally values are less than 1.3 mg/24 h metadrenaline, less than 20 µg adrenaline/24 h, and less than 8 µg noradrenaline/24 h.

LEAD INTOXICATION

Abdominal pain may be a prominent feature of lead poisoning. Measurement of serum lead is a readily available investigation, which is probably the best test. Another useful screening test is the demonstration of basophilic stippling of the erythrocytes. Quantitative estimations of the excretion of lead in the urine may be undertaken, and 0.2 mg/l is generally considered to be a significant concentration.

IMMUNOLOGY

This has had less impact on diagnosis than might have been expected. The *Widal test* remains a useful tool in typhoid, but is often difficult to interpret after immunisation. Specific salmonella serum antigen assay shows promise. *Lymphocyte function* and the absolute *numbers of B- and T-lymphocytes* circulation in the blood can be shown to be disturbed in various bowel diseases. Typing the *human leukocyte antigens* may be helpful. Of patients with coeliac disease 80% have HLA-A1 and -B8, and there is an increased frequency of HLA-B5 in Behçet's disease.

Coeliac disease

The *immunoglobulin pattern* is characteristic; the serum IgA level is low, normal or mildly raised, with low IgM and IgG levels. After gluten exclusion the IgA level tends to fall and a subsequent rise may indicate poor adherence to diet or lymphoma formation.

Endomysial antibodies appear to be a specific finding in patients with coeliac disease on a normal diet (and their relatives). They tend to disappear on gluten-free diets. *IgG-class reticulin antibodies* are found both in coeliac disease and inflammatory bowel disease.

Food allergy and intolerance

True food allergy is a contentious subject, and many alleged victims are suffering from psychiatric or other functional complaints.

The presence of *classic atopy*, especially with rhinitis and a positive family history, is a helpful clue to true food allergy. Atopy is often associated with *raised serum IgE levels,* which are up to 100 U/ml in normal adults and up to 50 U/ml in normal children. Blind allergen skin prick tests can be useful, but false positives are common.

Double blind challenge with suspected food allergens can provide objective evidence to support or refute diagnosis, but is very laborious and requires in-patient supervision to be effective. It may be reserved for patients whose symptoms improve or disappear with an open hypo-allergenic diet for a week (e.g. the water, lamb, rice and pears regime).

7

Large Bowel

RECTAL EXAMINATION

The rectal examination should form part of every complete physical examination. A measure of the importance of the rectal examination is gauged by the fact that about 15% of all large bowel cancers can be felt digitally. It is usually possible to reach further with a finger than can be seen with an anoscope.

Method

Before the examination proper the procedure is explained to the patient who is warned that there may be a desire to defecate. Many patients find this examination both embarrassing and uncomfortable, and they are considerably helped by a sympathetic and understanding attitude on the part of the examiner.

The patient is placed in the left lateral position with the head, trunk and hips well flexed. The buttocks are parted and the anal region inspected. The right index finger, covered by either a glove or finger cot, is well lubricated and inserted into the anus. It is advisable to use an anaesthetic jelly if a painful lesion such as a thrombosed haemorrhoid or fissure is suspected, and particular care is exercised in the introduction of the finger, which should be done very slowly. The examiner stands facing the patient's feet and introduces the finger from the posterior anal region. In the case of infants the little finger is used.

There are a number of other positions for rectal examination. In the left lateral position the left leg can be extended and the right thigh and knee flexed. The dorsal position is useful for a bimanual examination. The knee–chest position is convenient when a prostatic smear is being taken, though many patients find this posture fatiguing and embarrassing and it is not generally recommended.

The tone of the sphincter is noted, the anal muscle felt, and the finger is then introduced to the furthermost extent. It is then swept round in a full circle to examine the whole circumference of the rectum. The sacral curve, the lateral pelvic walls and the pubis are all palpated and the patient is requested to bear down to enable a further inch of the rectum to be palpated.

Particular note is made of the character of the prostate or the cervix and uterus. The female adenexae may be palpated by bimanual examination. An anal fissure may show as a tender linear ulcer. After withdrawing the finger the anus is cleaned. The material on the glove is examined and it can be used for microscopy and for testing for occult blood.

Interpretation

Cancer of the rectum will be felt as an indurated ulcerating lesion, a proliferating tumour or a stenosing infiltrative growth.

Rectal polyps can be very soft and may be mistaken for a mass of faeces, and a similar error can be made when palpating an amoeboma.

Internal haemorrhoids are not felt unless they are thrombosed, or are so large that they are felt as soft or 'wobbly' excrescences.

Crohn's disease of the rectum causes a nodular and indurated rectal wall.

Cancer of the prostate is identified by a 'rock-hard' prostate gland with or without fixation to the anterior rectal wall.

PROCTOSCOPY (ANOSCOPY)

The instrument commonly referred to as a proctoscope is more correctly termed an anal speculum or anoscope. It is used to visualise the anal mucosa and in no way replaces the digital or sigmoidoscopic examination. A variety of instruments is available and an instrument with a good light and a reasonably small diameter should be chosen. There are convenient transparent plastic disposable instruments. Informed consent should be obtained for these instrumental investigations, as with sigmoidoscopy and colonoscopy.

Method

The instrument is warmed in the examiner's hand or in warm water, and it is well lubricated using local anaesthetic jelly if necessary. The patient is reassured and warned about the sense of defecation. The proctoscope is gradually introduced into the anus with the patient in the left lateral position. The examiner stands facing the patient's feet, holding the handle of the proctoscope at the 12 o'clock position. The instrument is slowly inserted by a rotary clockwise movement so that a half circle has been described by the time the instrument is fully inserted. The handle now rests posteriorly between the gluteal folds. The obturator is withdrawn and an examination is made of the mucosa.

Interpretation

Details of mucosal changes in disease are given in the section dealing with the sigmoidoscope. Anoscopic examination is the best means of diagnosing internal haemorrhoids; the patient strains while the instrument is slowly withdrawn and the purplish vessels will be seen to bulge in the left lateral, right posterior and right anterior positions. Secondary, smaller, haemorrhoids may appear between these three primary positions. Other abnormalities to be seen include fissure, fistulas, anal and low rectal cancers, amoebic ulcers and proctitis.

SIGMOIDOSCOPY

Sigmoidoscopy is an integral part of the examination of the colon. It should always be performed before referring a patient for a barium enema examination. A number of instruments are available. For routine use a rigid 25 cm instrument (with a fibre-optic light source) is commonly used. Distal lighting systems have the disadvantage that they are more easily fouled and obscured, but they give superior illumination. Disposable instruments are now widely used.

There are 60 cm flexible fibre-optic and video sigmoidoscopes. They have the advantage that all the rectum and sigmoid colon can be seen and the descending colon is usually visible too. About 75% of large bowel cancers should be visible with this instrument. It is not certain at present whether the routine use of flexible sigmoidoscopy will reduce the need for colonoscopy, but flexible instruments are superior to rigid ones for examination of the distal large bowel. Informed consent should be obtained.

Method for rigid sigmoidoscopy

Preparation

The patient is reassured and warned that some discomfort might be felt, which can be alleviated to some extent by deep breathing. There may also be the desire to defecate. Normally no bowel preparation is necessary and the procedure can be undertaken readily on out-patients. Enemas and suppositories have the disadvantage that they alter the natural state of the mucous membrane, washing away secretions, and causing hyperaemia, which is an important consideration when the diagnosis of ulcerative colitis is being considered: enemas not only add to the difficulties of making a diagnosis but are potentially dangerous. It is reasonable to give a phosphate enema if a cancer of the colon is being considered and there is much faecal material. Various disposable enemas are available for out-patient use, but they may all cause mucosal irritation.

Position

The patient may be examined on a surgical table, or an examination couch, or in the hospital bed; in which instance it is helpful to place a fracture board under the mattress to ensure that the patient lies in the correct position. The examination is facilitated by being performed in a semi-darkened room. The left lateral position is preferred because it is more comfortable for the patient. For the sigmoidoscope to be successfully introduced, it is essential that the patient is correctly positioned. The patient is well flexed and lies transversely across the bed with the buttocks positioned at the very edge. The knees are slightly extended. A sandbag or pillow can be placed under the left hip, which is positioned at the edge of the couch. The left shoulder is tucked under the body and the right arm is brought forward. The head rests on a flat pillow. Failure to pass the sigmoidoscope fully is frequently the consequence of faulty positioning, particularly when the procedure is performed at the bedside. A soft mattress causes marked twisting of the spine, making it difficult to negotiate the curves in the rectum and lower colon. The position of the examiner is also important; he must be comfortable and relaxed and this is best achieved by either sitting on a low stool or kneeling at the bedside.

The knee–chest position may sometimes be helpful if there is much loose stool and blood, but is much less comfortable for the patient and is not recommended. In this position the knees are well drawn up and the back arched so that there is a distinct lumbar lordosis; the face is turned to one side, the chest and shoulders rest on the couch and the arms drop over the side of the couch.

Multi-purpose tables are available enabling the patient to be tilted into the knee–chest position.

Procedure

Before introducing the instrument the light connections are checked and the sigmoidoscope is warmed. It is lubricated and an anaesthetic jelly is used if necessary. A digital examination of the rectum is made and the patient warned that the instrument is about to be introduced.

The obturator is inserted in the sigmoidoscope and the instrument held in the right hand. It is introduced into the anus using a rotary movement and the tip is directed forwards for 5 cm in the direction of the umbilicus. The obturator is removed and the eye piece attached. From this point the examination is performed under direct vision. The instrument is now advanced in a backward direction and enters the rectum by following the curve of the sacrum. As the instrument is advanced it may become necessary to separate the mucosal folds by inflating with air, but this is kept to a minimum as it is both uncomfortable for the patient and potentially dangerous. Small pieces of stool usually can be moved out of the way with the end of the instrument; they are sometimes of value in indicating the position of the bowel lumen. Stool which occludes the end of the sigmoidoscope may be removed by introducing the obturator, withdrawing the instrument slightly and then removing the obturator. Another way is to displace the stool with a swab which is attached to a swab-holding forceps. Occasionally the forward passage of the instrument is prevented by spasm of the bowel, but if the sigmoidoscope is withdrawn slightly and held still for a short while, the spasm will disappear and it is possible to proceed with the examination.

The rectal mucosa is smooth and it is easy to see the rectal valves. The rectosigmoid junction is reached 12–15 cm from the anal margin. This is at the level of the sacral promontory and is identified by the change of the mucosa to concentric rugal folds. The rectosigmoid junction is usually sharply angled and may be difficult to transverse: the sigmoidoscope is directed anteriorly and to the right but the sharp angling may cause some discomfort. It may prove impossible to lever the proctosigmoidoscope through the rectosigmoid junction without undue discomfort. The sigmoid colon is not reliably reached without a general anaesthetic. The average penetration is 20 cm in men and 18.5 cm in women, but it is uncertain how far along the sigmoid colon the instrument passes, and it is probable that a mobile colon is simply displaced forwards. However, about 5 cm of the sigmoid may be seen. The instrument is now slowly withdrawn and the mucosa carefully rescrutin-ised and biopsies taken as required. After withdrawal of the instrument the patient is cleaned and any stool adhering to the sigmoidoscope is taken for examination. A full description of the procedure is entered in the patient's notes and this should include the distance to which the sigmoidoscope was introduced, the appearance of the mucosa, the presence of blood or mucus and the appearance of the stool, and whether a biopsy was taken and the site.

Method for flexible sigmoidoscopy

The equipment is conveniently mounted on a small trolley for out-patient use. The patient is prepared by phosphate purges or two phosphate enemas given simultaneously, which should normally clear the lower bowel in 30–45 min. The patient is positioned in the left lateral position with the knees flexed, and the lubricated tip of the instrument is advanced into the rectum. It is often necessary to withdraw the instrument a little to obtain a good view of the rectum. It is then possible to advance the instrument under direct vision, steering to keep the lumen in view at all times. With patience and gentle air insufflation it should be possible to view the entire rectum and sigmoid colon with only mild discomfort. Usually the descending colon can be seen also, and it may be possible to reach the splenic flexure or even enter the transverse colon, though unsedated patients do not always tolerate this. When patients are nervous, or where a full examination of the left colon is essential, or where a polypectomy is planned, it is preferable to conduct the procedure in a specialised investigation unit or as a day-ward case. This permits the use of midazolam i.v. to allow a complete passage of the 60 cm instrument to the splenic flexure. Suspect areas can be biopsied with endoscopy forceps: the largest compatible with the instrument are recommended.

Interpretation

When the mucous membrane is examined, an overall impression is obtained; particular attention is paid to the vascular pattern and whether there is bleeding, granularity, ulceration and oedema as judged by thickening of the rectal valves.

Normal

The mucous membrane is pink, it is not friable and should not bleed with the gentle passage of the instrument. Undue bleeding during the examination suggests that the mucosa is abnormal. The normal vascular pattern is well visualised and comprises a network of small arterioles and, to a lesser extent, venules. The rectal valves are sharp and crescentic in shape. A small amount of mucosa may be seen.

Ulcerative colitis and ulcerative proctitis

The appearances vary according to the stage of the disease. In the acute stage the mucosa is reddened, friable, haemorrhagic, and no vascular pattern can be seen. Thickening of the rectal valves almost to the point of obliteration indicates the presence of mucosal oedema. Ulcers are rarely distinguished and when seen appear shallow and irregular. There is nothing specific about these appearances which are to be seen in acute bacterial dysentery, occasionally in amoebic dysentery and in various toxic states. In the sub-acute and chronic stages of ulcerative colitis the normal vascular pattern is obscured, the mucosa is reddened and granular and bleeds readily when gently stroked by the sigmoidoscope or a swab. It is probable that some degree of mucosal abnormality such as excessive friability remains even with the most chronic and inactive of colonic involvement. Sigmoidoscopy is of value in distinguishing ulcerative colitis from ulcerative proctitis, in which only the terminal 10–12 cm of bowel is diseased.

Dysentery

The appearance is very similar in bacterial dysentery to that seen in acute ulcerative colitis. The mucosa in amoebic dysentery has small flask-shaped ulcers containing a small bead of pus, but is otherwise normal. However, the picture is variable and the mucous membrane may be quite reddened and inflamed and at times may present a picture not unlike acute ulcerative colitis.

Large bowel malignant disease

About half of all large bowel cancers may be seen with the rigid sigmoidoscope, and three-quarters with the flexible sigmoidoscope. Malignant growths are seen as infiltrating or ulcerating lesions with a varying amount of haemorrhage and necrosis. Other new growths include lobulated pink or red adenomatous polyps and sessile, branching soft villous adenomas. A neoplasm should be suspected if altered or fresh blood is seen in the lumen of the bowel ahead of the proctosigmoidoscope. Screening the population age 50–55 years with a flexible sigmoidoscopy has been proposed as an effective way of detecting early cancer.

Other diseases

Pneumatosis cystoides intestinalis shows as multiple glistening blue-purple submucous cysts.

Crohn's disease of the colon is difficult to distinguish from the other forms of colitis, but a nodular 'cobblestone' appearance of the mucosa with discrete ulcers suggests this disease. The rectum is less frequently involved in granulomatous than in ulcerative colitis.

In *diverticular disease* the mucosa may be reddened or normal, and the orifices of the diverticular will be seen with the flexible instrument.

A false impression of the colonic mucosa is obtained when suppositories or enemas are given prior to examination. The mucosa may become reddened and oedematous and appear very abnormal. Difficulties are also found in patients with severe diarrhoea from any cause because marked mucosal hyperaemia may be present in the absence of specific colonic disease.

RECTAL BIOPSY

This is a simple and safe procedure and instruments capable of obtaining a biopsy should always be available when a sigmoidoscopy is being performed.

Method (rigid instrument)

No anaesthetic is required if a biopsy is taken from the mucosa beyond the anal margin. A specimen is obtained from any growth that is seen, or from the mucosa itself, in which case it is easiest to biopsy one of the rectal valves, the uppermost being preferred. Many different biopsy forceps are available but unfortunately most are designed for biopsy tumours and it is not always possible to obtain good samples of the mucosa. A useful instrument is a 40 cm Chevalier Jackson (basket-shaped) forceps. This is introduced via the rigid proctosigmoidoscope and the area selected for biopsy is grasped. It is simple to catch a free margin of a rectal valve. The instrument is rotated gently to free the specimen and then withdrawn. The sample is removed from the forceps with a needle and gently unrolled, placed on filter paper and immersed in formol-saline. The biopsy site is inspected. Usually bleeding is slight and stops rapidly but it may be necessary to apply compression with a cotton wool swab. The sigmoidoscope is withdrawn and the patient warned that the next stool is likely to be bloodstained. Significant bleeding and perforation are uncommon complications. A few days should elapse between the taking of a biopsy and a barium enema examination.

Method (flexible instrument)

Biopsy forceps are passed through the channel to obtain samples, which are often smaller than those obtained with rigid equipment.

Interpretation

Careful attention to handling, processing, and sectioning is necessary to ensure accurate interpretation. Serial sections are cut perpendicular to the submucosal surface. Only the well-orientated sections are studied. Flattening the sample gently on a glass slide (or filter paper) prior to fixation assists optimal sectioning.

Normal

The glands are seen to be tubular and closely packed and the epithelium is columnar. There are numerous goblet cells. The lamina propria contains a moderate number of lymphocytes, plasma cells, reticuloendothelial cells and the occasional eosinophil. Variations within the normal range include slight dilatation or tortuosity of the glands, cuboidal surface epithelial cells and some increase in round cells in the lamina propria. The rectal glands are bulbous and shortened in specimens obtained from near the anal region.

Ulcerative colitis

In severe cases there is marked loss of glandular structure, extension mucosal ulceration with a heavy infiltration of cells particularly polymorphonuclear leukocytes, crypt abscesses, and a reduction in goblet cells and mucus. In moderate and mild inflammation there is oedema, dilatation of vessels, an occasional crypt abscess and superficial ulceration. There is an increase in lymphocytes, plasma cells and polymorphonuclear leukocytes. There is generally good correlation between the sigmoidoscopic and histological findings but this is not always so. The biopsy specimen is more likely to show inflammation when the sigmoidoscopic findings are normal than the reverse. Once the disease has developed, the mucosa remains permanently abnormal in the majority of patients whether or not symptoms are present. Biopsy samples obtained during a quiescent phase show a reduction in the number of rectal glands which tend to be bulbous, tortuous and branched. There is nothing specific about the mucosal biopsy in ulcerative colitis and all the features of the mucosal alterations in this disease may be found in colitis from other causes.

Rectal biopsies are valuable in the diagnosis of precancer dysplasia in patients with ulcerative colitis. There are two main types of abnormality: the polypoid variety, and precancerous change in a flat mucosa. *Polypoid precancerous changes* are recognised by the presence of multiple polyps which are usually sessile with a villous or papillary surface configuration. The villous growth pattern is the more significant. There is obvious inflammation in the lamina propria with loss of goblet cells. The nuclei are hyperchromatic with many mitotic figures. *Precancerous change in a flat mucosa* is more common. The mucosa is thicker and has a fairly nodular surface. The epithelial tubes are irregular in shape and size with lateral budding and a villous growth pattern. There is a tendency for the epithelial tubes to proliferate into the submucosa. A moderate amount of inflammatory cell infiltration is present. The implication of these histological features in the management of chronic ulcerative colitis remains uncertain, but generally is taken to require close surveillance and possibly elective colectomy if severe or progressive.

Crohn's disease of the colon

The mucosa is usually normal or shows non-specific inflammatory changes. It is helpful but unusual to find non-caseating giant-cell systems in the biopsy specimen.

Tumours

A papillary or villous *adenoma* will show a broad base with characteristic long papillary projections springing almost directly from the basement membrane. An adenomatous *polyp* shows focal glandular hyperplasia; there may be short papillary projections but there are always numerous glands below the surface epithelium and the villi do not extend to the submucosal base. The stalk is often fibromuscular in character. *Colonic cancers* are usually adenocarcinomas and less frequently colloid cancers.

Rectal biopsies have been used to in the diagnosis of amoebic colitis, schistosomiasis, amyloidosis, histiocytosis, some of the neurolipidoses and metachromatic leukodystrophy. *Hirschsprung's disease* can be detected with the use of special stains for nerve fibres and acetylcholinesterase activity, but requires deeper biopsies than usually can be safely obtained sigmoidoscopically.

Homosexual men often have non-specific cellular infiltration in the lamina propria, without pathological significance.

RADIOLOGY (Figures 20–22)

Radiological examination is still very important in the diagnosis of colonic disease, despite advances in endoscopic techniques.

Plain abdominal radiograph

The plain radiograph of the abdomen is helpful in acute, toxic ulcerative colitis when varying degrees of colonic dilatation may be seen as well as other

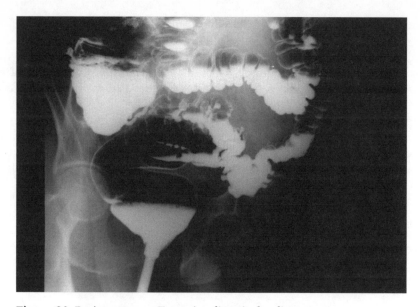

Figure 20 Barium enema. Extensive diverticular disease

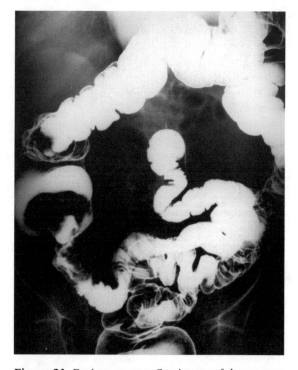

Figure 21 Barium enema. Carcinoma of the caecum

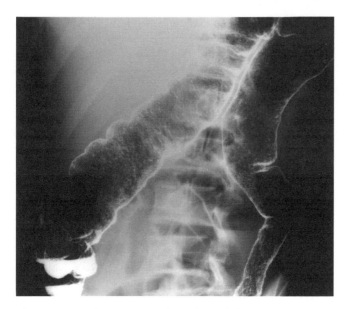

Figure 22 Barium enema. Ulcerative colitis

features of ulcerative colitis such as loss of haustrations and large pseudo-polyps. The site of a colonic cancer may be suspected when there is an abrupt end to the colonic gas shadow. In ischaemic colitis there may be gas in abnormal sites, such as the bowel wall, and evidence of mucosal oedema ('thumb-printing'). A technique of insufflation of 500–800 ml air has been described as safe and useful in acute colitis – the 'air enema'.

Barium enema

A barium enema is usually required in the diagnosis of disease in the colon. It is important that the radiologist is given ample clinical information, particularly when ulcerative colitis or diverticulitis is suspected, because the technique of preparation and examination may have to be modified. As a rule a barium enema should not be performed in acute ulcerative colitis or acute diverticulitis. The examination is not without danger, and it can exacerbate the colitis or cause a perforation of an acutely inflamed bowel. When a barium enema is performed it should routinely include air-contrast studies because these give far superior results and leave fewer uncertainties to be resolved by colonoscopy.

Table 2 Simple clinical colitis activity index

		Score
Bowel frequency		
Day	1–3	0
	4–6	1
	7–9	2
	>9	3
Night	1–3	1
	4–6	2
Urgency of defecation	hurry	1
	immediately	2
	incontinence	3
Blood in stool	trace	1
	occasionally frank	2
	usually frank	3
General well-being	very well	0
	slightly below par	1
	poor	2
	very poor	3
	terrible	4
Extracolonic features		1 each
	Maximum score	13+

Interpretation

Ulcerative colitis

There are fine serrations along the bowel margin, loss of haustrations, pseudo-polyps and extensive undermining of the mucosa. In long-standing disease there may be loss of haustrations, marked shortening of the bowel and rigidity producing the typical 'hose-pipe' colon. On the other hand the radiographic appearances may be virtually normal. In mild colitis flattening and blunting of the haustration give a 'corrugated' appearance. It must be remembered that a normal colon may have no haustration distal to the splenic flexure. Changes in the rectum of diagnostic value include thickening and irregularity of the mucosal folds, small ulcerations, and contraction of the rectal wall. There is an increase in the retrorectal soft tissue space which is greater than 10 mm. A barium enema is of value in determining the extent of the colonic involvement in ulcerative colitis.

While there is a good correlation in general between the colonoscopic, histological and radiological findings in this disease, this is not always so. Disease defined by colonoscopy tends to be more extensive than that seen by radiology. It is advisable that the diagnosis of ulcerative colitis be made on the basis of all three investigations. Regrettably, if the barium enema demonstrates a carcinoma superimposed upon ulcerative colitis it is usually only at a fairly advanced stage of growth.

Crohn's colitis

At an early stage there are ileal and caecal impressions due to swollen lymph nodes at the ileocaecal junction. A reversible narrowing of the colonic lumen may be associated with small ulcers. At a more advanced stage the involvement is seen to be segmental, there is thickening and blunting of the mucosal folds with asymmetrical involvement. Inflammatory polyps, linear and transverse ulcerations, pseudo-diverticula and stricture formation may all be seen. Characteristically, the right side of the colon is more frequently involved than the left. However, Crohn's disease may closely mimic ulcerative colitis.

Neoplasms

In the colon these appear as cicatrising lesions or as proliferating 'polypoid' growths. The incidence of false-negative diagnosis in cancer of the colon (excluding the rectum) is about 10%. The site of the cancer determines to some extent whether or not it is detected. Growths in the rectum and at the rectosigmoid junction are particularly difficult to see, and associated diverticular disease adds to the difficulties. The Malmö technique, a modification of the double-contrast method in which special attention is given to direct preparation of the colon, has a very high detection rate for colonic polypoid tumours.

Other diseases

Diverticular disease. The diverticula usually fill with barium. A jagged 'sawtooth' appearance with apparently marked mucosal distortion represents failure of the colon to elongate because of muscle hypertrophy and is not evidence of inflammation. When inflammation is present there is narrowing, rigidity and intramural sinus tracts.

In the chronic stages of *ischaemic colitis* a stricture may be seen which characteristically involves the splenic flexure. The bowel may show a scalloped edge with mucosal irregularity, sacculation and tubular narrowing.

In acute *amoebiasis* shallow ulcers may be demonstrated and the appearances are those of ulcerative colitis. In the more chronic phase a contracted caecum may be seen or an amoeboma filling defect, usually in the caecum or rectum. This condition is not usually diagnosed by radiology.

Cathartic colon. This shows an absence of normal haustral markings, a smooth bowel wall with no irregularity, no thickening of the bowel and, very characteristically, pseudostrictures which are tapering, transient contractions.

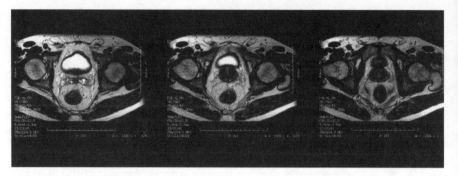

Figure 23 Magnetic resonance imaging (MRI). Carcinoma of the rectum

The changes are found initially in the right side of the colon. Proctosigmoid-oscopic demonstration of melanosis colic confirms the aetiology.

CT scanning

This has been proposed especially in the elderly as a practical alternative to barium enema. It is possible to process images to give a virtual reality image of the colon.

Magnetic resonance imaging (MRI) (Figure 23)

This can be useful for staging rectal and pelvic tumours

Arteriography

This has enjoyed a resurgence with the appreciation of the great frequency with which angiodysplasia of the right side of the colon causes rectal bleeding in the elderly. Rapid serial radiographs are taken over 30 s, after injection of contrast medium into the superior mesenteric artery. Arterial, capillary and venous phases of filling are demonstrated. In angiodysplasia there are small clusters of arteries on the antimesenteric border or the caecum and the ascending colon, intense capillary filling, and early, intense and prolonged pacifications of the veins.

Arteriography can diagnose and localise tumours of the colon, but it has largely been superseded by colonoscopy for this purpose.

ULTRASONOGRAPHY

External ultrasound has been used to identify acute appendicitis and, after fluid-filling, to examine the whole colon. Of more practical importance is the use of rectal probes to investigate rectal and prostatic cancer.

COLONOSCOPY

The essentials for adequate examination are a clean colon and a co-operative patient. If these conditions are met it is possible to examine fully the left side of the colon in almost every patient, and in 70% or more of examinations the caecum is reached. The procedure is, however, difficult and time-consuming. Success depends on operator experience, and it is common for the initial examinations by an investigator to be very frustrating. Informed consent should be obtained.

Instruments

There is a range of lengths of instruments. Among the most useful are those of length 160 cm. These have a single biopsy and suction channel. If it is only desired to inspect the sigmoid and descending colon then 60 cm sigmoidoscopes are better as they are more easily manoeuvred. Biopsy forceps are available for the various colonoscopes. Other useful accessories include a diathermy snare and polyp-grasping forceps.

Preparation (Golytely)

A safe technique involves the use of oral lavage. Usually the preparation 'Klean Prep' to 4 litres is used. Alternatively a solution is made up with sodium sulphate and polyethylene glycol (80 mM) to give an electrolyte concentration in mEq/l of: Na 125; K 10; SO_4 80; Cl 35; HCO_3 20. This may be flavoured and 2.5–4.0 litres are drunk. Alternatively a nasogastric tube is passed and the patient is placed on a comfortable lavatory seat. The solution is then infused at 20–30 ml/min, and purgation is complete in 3 h. This preparation is rapid and obviates the need for any preliminaries before the day of colonoscopy. The solution used is stated not to permit any appreciable net fluid secretion or absorption in the intestine.

A lower volume oral sodium phosphate preparation has been introduced (Phospho-Soda). Experience of safety and efficacy are less extensive.

Physiological saline and mannitol purges proved hazardous and they should not be used. No preparation is needed with brisk bleeding, when the bowel is often empty of faeces.

Procedure

The patient is positioned in the left lateral position with the knees drawn up and the buttocks on the edge of the bed. Oximetry is desirable.

A rectal examination is performed to ensure that there are no faeces present. Midazolam 5 mg and pethidine 50 mg i.v. are given slowly. The dose may need reduction in the elderly or respiratory invalid, and naloxone 400 µg and flumazenil 500 µg should be available to reverse excess sedation. The lubricated instrument is introduced into the rectum and the light switched on to visualise the mucosa. If the bowel lumen is not clearly seen, gentle air insufflation and withdrawal are helpful. The view may be partly obscured by traces of residual faeces or enema, but it is not worthwhile trying to clear the field completely. The lumen is followed as far as possible, using the directional controls, torsion and withdrawal. If the lumen cannot be brought into view, progress can nonetheless be made by 'sliding by' the mucosa, but should the mucosa blanch or fail to move past the lens the instrument should be withdrawn a little.

The *sigmoid colon* is tortuous and navigation is especially difficult in the presence of diverticular disease. Loops may be formed which prevent progress even when the lumen is well in view. Torsion and withdrawal usually improves the position.

Once the *descending colon* is reached it is usually possible to straighten out the sigmoid colon by judicious withdrawal and making the sigmoid colon concertina on the instrument. The success of this manoeuvre can be checked by rolling the patient on to the back and visualising the position of the colonoscope using the image intensifier.

In cases of difficulty in negotiating the sigmoid colon the 'alpha loop' manoeuvre may be helpful. The instrument is withdrawn to the lower sigmoid and the colonoscope twisted to 180 degrees anticlockwise before further entry. This creates a single spiral in the sigmoid and permits further passage up into the descending colon. The loop must be undone by clockwise rotation when the tip is in the descending colon.

The descending colon is straight and usually traversed with ease. The *splenic flexure* is variable in conformity; it may be passed readily but often it is a sharp angle which necessitates much manipulation and air insufflation for passage. The dusky purplish appearance of the spleen and/or liver may be seen through the upper part of the splenic flexure and is a helpful landmark. The *transverse colon* is triangular in shape and freely mobile. It is possible to stretch the bowel without making progress, in which event the instrument should be cautiously withdrawn, whereupon paradoxical advance of the tip is often seen. The *hepatic flexure* can be identified by the purplish appearance of the adjacent liver, but this part of the bowel is even more variable than the splenic flexure and may be passed without being identified. The *ascending colon* is quite short and easily negotiated. If it appears that there is insufficient length of instrument to pass the whole colon, it is helpful to withdraw and suck out air. The *caecum* is recognised by the fact that it is a cul-de-sac, often with prominent folds. It contains the ileocaecal valve and appendix orifice, but neither of these is invariably seen, and it is useful to confirm by fluoroscopy that the whole colon has been passed. A non-radiological magnetic imaging technique has also been described. It is sometimes possible to enter the terminal ileum. The mucosa is inspected during withdrawal of the instrument and in order to avoid loops rushing by the tip of the endoscope it should be removed gradually.

Interpretation

Inflammatory bowel disease can be classified by colonoscopy according to its extent and severity. In *ulcerative colitis* there is a uniform inflammation of the mucosa which almost always affects the rectum and spreads proximally continuously. Frank bleeding may be seen, but the separate ulcers are too small to identify. In *Crohn's disease* similar appearances can occur, but often there are discrete ulcers with relatively normal mucosa in between. Rectal spasm and discontinuous disease are common in Crohn's colitis. *Amoebiasis* appears as raised ulcers overlying small amoebic abscesses.

Diverticular disease causes problems in passing the sigmoid colon, which is tortuous and with prominent circular muscles. The mouths of the diverticula can usually be identified and sometimes may be so large as to simulate the bowel lumen.

Vascular abnormalities (angiodysplasias) generally on the right side of the colon are increasingly being recognised as a cause of rectal bleeding in the elderly. They are seen as small leashes of vessels and venous lakes.

Strictures and carcinomas are usually easily recognised; biopsies should always be taken.

Polyps are a very common finding. Small 2–3 mm, sessile metaplastic polyps are common and of no significance. Larger and pedunculated polyps should be biopsied or removed by diathermy snare. In practice it is only polyps greater than 10 mm in diameter which are likely to be malignant.

If the diathermy snare is used it is important to lift the polyp away from the bowel wall and to ensure that there is no persistent local bleeding. The separated polyp is retrieved by forceps and submitted to histology.

Indications

(1) Evaluation and biopsy of strictures and polyps suspected of malignancy.
(2) Assessment of the extent and nature of inflammatory bowel disease.
(3) Determination of the cause of rectal bleeding, either as an immediate investigation or when barium enema has been unhelpful.
(4) Assessment of post-operative appearances, for example recurrence and activity of inflammatory bowel disease prior to anastomosis.
(5) Diagnostic and therapeutic polypectomy without laparotomy.
(6) Identification of luminal lesions at open surgery.
(7) Exclusion of multiple diseases, e.g. inflammatory bowel disease and co-existing diverticular disease.
(8) Confirmation of ischaemic colitis.
(9) Inspection of the terminal ileum in suspected Crohn's disease.

Cleaning

Cleaning and sterilisation are performed in a manner similar to that used for upper digestive endoscopes. Thorough washing is essential and a very soft toothbrush or cotton buds are helpful in cleaning the lens.

IMMUNOLOGY

Inflammatory bowel disease

Despite the probable disorder of immune mechanisms present in ulcerative colitis and Crohn's disease, immunological studies have not proved useful in diagnosis. Fifteen percent of patients with ulcerative colitis have antibodies to colonic epithelial cell cytoplasm, and in rather more there are IgG-class antireticulin antibodies. Patients with associated liver disease may have smooth muscle, nuclear, ANCA and mitochondrial antibodies. A high frequency of the human leukocyte antigen HLA-B27 is observed when ankylosing spondylitis occurs in association with inflammatory bowel disease. Haemagglutinating antibodies can be found, especially in children, and are not necessarily linked with autoimmune haemolytic anaemia. The acute phase reactant alpha-acid glycoprotein (seromucoid) and haptoglobin are elevated in ulcerative colitis, and this correlates with clinical activity of the disease. By contrast, pre-albumin tends to fall in active ulcerative colitis.

Carcinoembryonic antigen(CEA)

This glycoprotein was first found in tumour tissue from patients with large bowel cancer, and it was later shown to be present in serum as well.

It is detected in 50–90% of patients with large bowel cancer. When an upper limit of normal of 5 µmol/l is set, only 1.1% of healthy non-smoking individuals have CEA in their serum. However, it is commonly found in apparently healthy smokers in the range 5–17 µmol/l, and also in patients with carcinomas of the lung, pancreas and gastrointestinal tract, in severe alcoholic liver disease and in anaemia. It therefore has limited value as a screening test.

CEA levels usually fall to normal in patients whose large bowel carcinoma has been completely resected and who have no metastases. A subsequent rise in titre indicates recurrent tumour, and this can be detected months before clinical recurrence. Falls in CEA levels correlate with objective response to chemotherapy in 75% of patients.

Monoclonal antibodies are under evaluation for tumour localisation.

Amoebiasis

Entamoeba histolytica infection may be symptomatic, or it may cause dysentery and liver abscesses. The stool should be examined for motile amoebae and

Table 3 Diagnosis of amoebiasis

	Positive %	
	GDP	IHA
Amoebic liver abscess	85	95
Amoebic colitis	91	95
Other diarrhoea or liver abscesses	1	5
After effective treatment	Usually becomes negative at 6 months	Remains positive

cysts, and proctosigmoidoscopy can show typical appearances and yield diagnostic histology. However, there is often difficulty in confirming a diagnosis, and serology can be very helpful. A complement fixation test is available. It is not as helpful as indirect haemoagglutination (IHA) and gel diffusion precipitation (GDP), and a combination of these two is used diagnostically. The use of serology for galactose-inhabitable adherence protein is said to be 99% sensitive, and may become the technique of choice.

E. histolytica may be an innocent commensal, especially in the homosexual male, and zymodeme typing by electrophoresis is useful to assess pathogenicity.

8

Gastrointestinal Bleeding

Bleeding from the alimentary tract may present as an unexplained anaemia, as the passage of black stool, as the passage of red blood per rectum, or by vomiting of fresh or altered blood.

The investigation of gastrointestinal bleeding involves answering two major questions: (1) is the patient still bleeding? and (2) where is the bleeding site?

Frank bleeding from the upper gastrointestinal tract, that is, a site proximal to the duodeno–jejunal junction or ligament of Treitz, is usually obvious, presenting as a haematemesis or melaena stools. Fresh blood in the stools usually indicates rectal or colonic disease. However, it is possible for a bleeding lesion in the upper gastrointestinal tract to present with the passage of red blood per rectum; similarly a bleeding lesion in the caecum or ascending colon may cause melaena stools. The factors determining the degree of alteration of the blood in the gut include the site of the bleeding, the amount of blood lost and the motility of the bowel.

OCCULT BLOOD TESTS

Between 100 and 200 ml of blood in the gut is necessary to produce a tarry stool. With smaller volumes the stools are normally coloured and special tests are necessary to detect the presence of blood. Tests for occult blood are either used to detect the cause of an iron deficiency anaemia or to help in the diagnosis of those lesions of the gut which are frequently associated with bleeding such as peptic ulcer, carcinoma and polyps. An average of 0.7 ml/day of blood is normally lost in the gastrointestinal tract.

Chemical tests are in universal use because of their simplicity, but it is extremely difficult to devise a standard chemical test which is neither too sensitive nor too insensitive.

Faecal samples for testing may be obtained from a stool sample, which is best taken from within a lump of faeces on the glove after rectal examination. It is possible by vigorous digital examination to cause sufficient trauma to the rectal mucosa to give a positive test for blood in the stool, so that a gentle examination is essential when procuring a sample of faeces for chemical examination.

There is a variety of commercial tests available. They are based on peroxidase-like activity in haemoglobin which causes the reagent used to develop a blue colour reaction. The most convenient sensitive test available is the guaiac test Hemachek, which is supplied as a kit so that the patient may send his/her own samples by post for examination. A specimen of stool is smeared on filter paper in a card. The reagent is added in the laboratory and a blue coloration indicates the presence of blood in the stool. This method reliably detects amounts of bleeding of 10 ml or more daily, and usually gives positive results if there is a loss of more than 2.5 ml daily. Haemoccult is a very much less sensitive guaiac test.

The Fecatwin system depends on two levels of sensitivity for guaiac testing, with additional confirmation of the presence of human haemoglobin by an immunological technique. It is rather too elaborate for routine use.

False-positive reactions

The main objection to sensitive tests is the occurrence of false-positive reactions. These reactions are almost exclusively dietary in origin originating from the ingestion of red meat, uncooked vegetables, unboiled milk and fruit such as bananas. Opinions differ as to whether or not oral iron preparations can produce positive results, but it is probable that a weakly positive result may follow the ingestion of ferrous compounds.

Negative occult blood tests do not exclude ulcerative or neoplastic lesions of the gastrointestinal tract.

The role of occult blood testing in *screening ostensibly healthy subjects* is controversial, but it has been used to detect early large bowel cancer.

Where patients give a history consistent with *gastrointestinal bleeding*, or are being investigated for iron deficiency anaemia or suspected gastrointestinal disease, a different approach is used.

(1) Haemorrhoids, gingivitis and epistaxis are excluded.
(2) Drugs, such as aspirin, which cause gastrointestinal bleeding are stopped.
(3) Three separate stool samples are tested by routine methods – a significant result is two or three positive

In practice, barium radiology and endoscopy are necessary in the diagnosis of difficult cases.

There is usually little doubt as to whether there is fresh blood in vomit. When altered blood or coloured material is present there may be uncertainty and the tests for occult blood mentioned above may be applied to gastric aspirate or vomit. 'Coffee ground' vomit is not proven haematemesis until shown to contain blood in this way.

ISOTOPE TESTS

Technetium colloid test

When bleeding is brisk, then simple i.v. injection of ^{99m}Tc-colloid and scanning the abdomen shortly afterwards can localise sites of haemorrhage.

Radio-labelled erythrocytes

Localisation of sites of GI bleeding is not always possible with endoscopy and radiology, and scanning after injection of ^{99m}Tc-labelled red cells is often helpful.

Method

Patients are pretreated with 1 mg i.v. stannous chloride. Twenty minutes later a heparinised syringe containing ^{99m}Tc-pertechnetate is attached to an intravenous cannula and 5 ml blood withdrawn into it. The whole blood is incubated in the syringe with the radio-label at room temperature for 10 min then re-injected. Gamma camera scanning of the abdomen is then undertaken. For more rapid bleeding sites, scanning every 5 min for 30 min then at 1 and 2 h will normally locate the site. If possible, lateral and oblique images are made as well as anterior ones, to give a 3D representation. For recurrent bleeding or when the initial images were negative then a 24-h scan is performed.

Interpretation

Focal accumulation of isotope indicates a bleeding site, but a negative investigation does not exclude it. The test is most useful for large bowel sites of bleeding, but can also be helpful in the small intestine.

^{99m}Tc-pertechnetate scanning

Where Meckel's diverticulum is suspected, especially in children, this test will locate the gastric heterotopia.

OTHER TESTS

Radiology (Figure 24)

Barium meal and follow-through, small bowel enema and a barium enema are all sometimes useful in the investigation of gastrointestinal bleeding. Barium enemas should be by the double-contrast technique unless there is a specific contraindication.

The demonstration of a lesion does not prove that it is the bleeding site. This applies particularly to sigmoid diverticula. It is extremely difficult to decide upon the site of bleeding when two lesions are demonstrated, for example oesophageal varices and peptic ulcer. Portography may be performed when oesophageal and gastric varices are suspected. Arteriography is used to demonstrate lesions such as vascular anomalies, ulcers and neoplasia, and has been particularly recommended in the diagnosis of caecal tumours. Arteriography has also been used with success in the location of acute

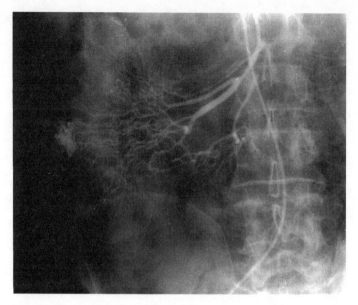

Figure 24 Selective superior mesenteric angiogram. Active bleeding in the ascending colon

gastrointestinal haemorrhage by observing the site at which the dye leaks into the bowel lumen; it can be used to diagnose bleeding oesophageal varices.

Endoscopy

Upper digestive endoscopy, sigmoidoscopy and colonoscopy may all be required to determine the site of bleeding. Endoscopy is helpful because it may demonstrate that a lesion is actually bleeding. The performance of upper digestive endoscopy within 24 h for admission with haematemesis greatly improves the diagnosis rate.

Enteroscopy

Equipment

The small intestine may be examined with longer endoscopes than used for oesophago-gastro-duodenoscopy. Both video and fibre-optic equipment is available. Fluoroscopic screening will identify the extent of examination. If push equipment is used then i.v. midazolam and pethidine make the procedure more comfortable.

Dedicated instruments about 2 m long are available. They are passed in the same way as a pan-endoscope then advanced slowly into the distal duodenum and jejunum under direct vision. Because of the tendency to loop in the stomach, over-tubes have been devised to speed passage. Loops of bowel can be made to concertina in the instrument, although the ileum is not always reached. The bowel is carefully inspected on withdrawal. Both paediatric and adult colonoscopes have been successfully used in departments which do not possess a dedicated enteroscope.

Indications

(1) Obscure GI bleeding where gastroscopy, colonoscopy and barium enema are negative. Typical findings are angiodysplasia, and tumours which may be biopsied.
(2) Anaemia and other GI symptoms in patients on long-term NSAID therapy. Small bowel ulcers and diaphragms may be seen.
(3) Evaluation of extent and severity of Crohn's disease.
(4) Treatment by laser therapy of bleeding sites and balloon dilation of strictures.

GASTROINTESTINAL BLEEDING IN LIVER DISEASE

If a patient is suspected to be bleeding from oesophageal varices, the sooner the correct diagnosis is made the more promptly appropriate therapy can be given. If varices are known to be present, then the early use of terlipressin may be the best policy. However, it is preferable to obtain an urgent endoscopy since other lesions commonly bleed even in the patient with varices. Also, early endoscopy permits therapeutic procedures such as banding or injection of varices, and injection of peptic ulcers.

9

Stool Examination

MACROSCOPIC APPEARANCE

Normally the stool is firm or semi-formed and is coloured varying shades of brown. It may be possible to recognise undigested food particles and their frequency reflects the nature of the diet, the amount of mastication and the degree of intestinal hurry. The shape of the stool varies greatly and is of little diagnostic significance.

Blood from anorectal diseases is seen as streaks on the surface of the stool. Blood from lesions higher up the colon will be intimately mixed with the stool as is characteristically found in inflammatory bowel disease. The passage of pure blood with no faecal material may occur with polyps, haemorrhoids, colonic cancer, diverticular disease, infarction of the colon and intussusception. Patients with bleeding peptic ulcers occasionally pass bright red, unaltered blood per rectum. The stools may be coloured red after the ingestion of beetroot.

The stools are pale where there is intra- and extra-hepatic cholestasis and in severe steatorrhoea. Tarry black melaena stools indicate the partial digestion of blood in the gastrointestinal tract. The appearance is usually characteristic, but if there is any doubt the stool is mixed with a small volume of water which will be coloured red. Chemical tests for blood should be performed. Iron-containing stools are grey-black and can usually be distinguished from melaena. Other causes of black stools include the ingestion of charcoal, bismuth compounds and large quantities of liquorice.

PROTOZOA AND HELMINTHS

Various intestinal parasites may be seen by the naked eye in the stool including tapeworms (*Taenia solium* or *saginata*), roundworms *(Ascaris lumbricoides)*, and threadworms *(Enterobius vermicularis)*.

It may be necessary to undertake repeated examinations of the stool. Stools should always be collected and examined before a barium examination. Commercial stool collection kits are available which contain preservatives for parasites and cysts.

A microscopic examination of a stool suspension is required to diagnose pathogenic protozoa and helminthic ova. Stool can be obtained from a bedpan or other container; alternatively it is possible to use the material off the glove after performing a rectal examination. A wooden applicator is used to place a pea-sized portion of stool on a microscope dish previously moistened with two or three drops of isotonic saline. A coverslip is applied carefully to ensure that no air bubbles are trapped. The slide is scanned under low power, and particularly at the edges. *Entamoeba histolytica* and *Escherichia coli* can exist in vegetative and multinucleate cystic forms; the biflagellate *Giardia intestinalis* may be identified, although it is more readily found in the duodenal aspirate; and *Enterobius vermicularis* can be demonstrated. Ova which may be seen include *Ascaris lumbricoides, Ankylostoma duodenale, Necator americanus, Taenia saginata, Taenia solium, Enterobius vermicularis,* and *Strongyloides stercoralis.*

Enterobiasis (seatworm, pinworm or threadworm, *E. vermicularis*)

This condition is not usually diagnosed from an examination of the stools because the adult female parasite is seldom longer than 10 mm and the stools contain ova in only 10% of infected patients. The usual method of diagnosis is to obtain ova from the perianal skin using the transparent adhesive tape test. This test is performed preferably in the early morning and can be undertaken by parents on their children. The terminal 10 mm of a length of clear, transparent adhesive tape is pressed on one end of a microscopic slide. The rest of the tape is folded backwards with the sticky surface facing outward. The slide is directed gently into the anal verge so that the sticky surface of the tape touches the anus and immediate perianal area. The slide is then removed and the tape flipped over so that the adhesive surface attaches to the slide. The tape is smoothed over carefully using tissue paper in order to remove air bubbles and wrinkles. The slide is examined under the microscope.

Amoebiasis

The search for amoebae must be made before the patient undergoes a course of antimicrobial treatment, especially metronidazole. Similarly a barium enema renders the stool unsuitable for the diagnosis of amoebiasis. On the other hand, a dose of penicillin has been used to 'chase' the amoebae into the stool, increasing the chance of finding the trophozoites in the faeces.

Only fresh warm stool is examined. Material obtained at the time of sigmoidoscopy may also be used. A 'button' of faeces is emulsified on a slide in a drop of warm normal saline. The slide may be kept warm by heating on the microscope lamp. The preparation is examined under the low power magnification. The amoebae and their multinucleate cysts are seen as refractile objects which are examined in greater detail under the high power magnification. Trophozoites of *E. histolytica* are most likely to be found in mucus and cysts are found in the more solid parts of the stool.

Hanging drop preparation

If the faecal suspension is applied carefully to the lower surface of a warmed slide, amoebic motility may be more readily observed. The examination is made by focusing up and down.

Both amoebiasis and giardiasis are more frequent in male homosexuals; 40% are infected with either or both. In HIV disease crytosporidial diarrhoea is common. AIDS also commonly presents as upper GI candida and sometimes as hepatitis, as well as with weight loss.

BACTERIA

A sample of freshly-passed stool is taken with a disposable wooden spatula and placed in a screwtop container. The stool must be free of urine. Disposable containers with plastic spatulas attached to the lid are also convenient sampling devices. The stool should be delivered to the laboratory on the day it is passed. If amoebic dysentery is suspected a warm sample of stool should be examined immediately after the specimen has been obtained.

Alternative procedures are to take stool from the glove or proctosigmoidoscope after internal examination. Rectal swabs may be useful but it is important that they are taken from the rectum and not the perineum. This requires passage of a proctoscope.

Samples should be cultured in a solid selective and a liquid enrichment medium, with body aerobic and anaerobic culture. A single negative culture does not exclude infection, and normally two stool samples should be sent. However, any positive results are usually obtained with the first sample. Some individuals are asymptomatic carriers of organisms.

Bacteria which are traditionally more important in diarrhoeal illnesses are *Salmonella, Shigella and Staphylococcus*. Some strains of *Escherichia coli* (e.g. 0157) are pathogenic.

Patients with *Salmonella* or *Shigella* in the stool usually have diarrhoea persisting over 24 h, fever, blood in the stool, abdominal pain and nausea. In the absence of all of these features, stool culture is frequently negative, and random stool cultures in patients presenting with diarrhoea are infrequently rewarding. Serology by ELISA may be more satisfactory for *Salmonella enteritis*.

Campylobacter and *Clostridium difficile* are other causes of enterocolitis. *C. difficile* infection is particularly important as it may follow antibacterial therapy. It is a fastidious anaerobe which produces a cytopathic enterotoxin that can be identified in stool. Infection is one of the few diarrhoeas needing specific antibacterial therapy.

VIRUSES

Many apparently infective diarrhoeas cannot be ascribed to a specific organism. They are commonly attributed to viral infection, although this is rarely proved. Examination of *paired sera* taken during the first acute illness and then 2–4 weeks later may show diagnostic elevation of titres of antibodies to viruses such as the *Coxsackie group*.

Rotavirus infection is common in children and clumped virions may be found after low-speed centrifugation of stool suspensions. Virus particles are concentrated with a selectively absorbent hydrophilic gel prior to diagnostic electron microscopy.

Electron microscopy may also reveal the presence of other viruses, in particular the 29-nm RNA particles of *Hepatitis type A*.

10

Pancreas

The investigation for pancreatic disease remains problematical and unsatisfactory, despite the introduction of a host of techniques. The use of endoscopic retrograde cholangiopancreatography (ERCP), ultrasonography, computed tomography (CT) or magnetic resonance imaging (MRI) to define the anatomy of the gland, coupled with one of the tests of exocrine secretion are probably the most satisfactory methods of assessment. Estimation of steatorrhoea, glucose tolerance and serum amylase can provide valuable additional information. These tests are required to decide whether pancreatic disease is present, and if so to determine its nature. The differentiation of chronic pancreatitis from pancreatic cancer is an important though often unresolved question. The laboratory diagnosis of pancreatic disease can be quite simple in the presence of jaundice, glycosuria or steatorrhoea; it is when the only symptom is abdominal pain that the diagnosis frequently proves extremely difficult.

ULTRASONOGRAPHY (US) (Figures 25, 26)

Procedures are operator dependent, but the test is non-invasive and in experienced hands the results are accurate.

Fasting patients are examined in three main positions: prone, lateral decubitus, and supine. This permits full visualisation of the whole pancreas. Sometimes effervescent preparations are necessary to fill the stomach with gas and enhance contrast. A complete record with serial transverse and sagittal sections takes about 1 h to complete. The simultaneous use of ultrasonic scanning permits fine-needle aspiration of pancreatic lesions for cytological examination. The best results may be obtained by ultrasound-guided percutaneous biopsy using the automatic firing 18 gauge needle (Biopty gun).

Endosonography

This is promoted as the ideal approach to US appraisal of the pancreas. It permits needle biopsy. However, the equipment is very expensive, the procedure requires much expertise, and it is not generally available at present.

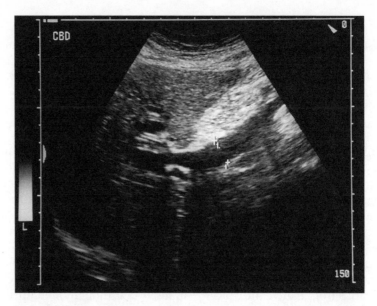

Figure 25 Ultrasonogram. Dilated pancreatic duct in carcinoma of the head of the pancreas

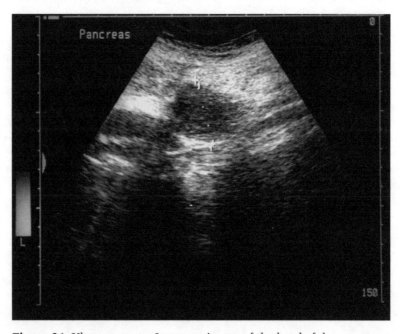

Figure 26 Ultrasonogram. Large carcinoma of the head of the pancreas

Interpretation

Normal pancreas reflects few echoes, and interference from other structures, gaseous distension and obesity, can be a problem. The gland may be difficult to locate because of its small size and variable position. It can be identified in about 80% of individuals.

Acute pancreatitis. The thickness of the pancreas increases to about twice normal and the parenchymal echoes lessen or disappear. More importantly, the development of abscesses and pseudocysts can be readily detected in acute pancreatitis, and their progress followed by serial scans. The pancreatic scan is abnormal in 58% of patients with acute pancreatitis, and in as many as 92% whose symptoms and signs suggest a *pseudocyst*, when ultrasonography is the best method for diagnosis.

Chronic pancreatitis. The gland often, but not always, enlarges, and irregular areas of high and low echoes are characteristic. Calcification gives scattered foci of dense echoes, and this can be detected in about one-third of patients. Positive scans are more often found during clinical relapse. Pancreatic duct abnormalities associated with chronic pancreatitis may be detectable; an increase in calibre up to 2 cm can be found. Although a diagnostic accuracy of 65–94% can be achieved in chronic pancreatitis, the method is not entirely foolproof because carcinoma of the pancreas may give similar changes.

Pancreatic carcinoma. This can be recognised in about 85% of cases as a well-defined tumour with few internal echoes. Growths above 12 mm should be detected, but there is often associated enlargement of the gland or chronic pancreatitis which makes interpretation more difficult. It is easier to diagnose tumours in the body and tail than in the head of the pancreas.

Hepatic metastases can be detected in most cases where they are present.

Obstructive jaundice. Ultrasonography should detect dilated extrahepatic ducts in 95% of cases, and when the cause lies in the pancreas its nature can be defined in the vast majority of patients.

Indications

(1) First investigation for chronic disease where the pancreas is under suspicion.
(2) First investigation for cholestatic jaundice (in association with hepato-biliary scans).
(3) Diagnosis of pancreatic pseudocysts and abscesses.
(4) Diagnosis and monitoring acute pancreatitis.
(5) Guiding percutaneous pancreatic biopsy

Computed tomography is definitely superior to ultrasound for non-invasive investigation of morphology, and if freely available should always be considered in case of difficulty. It is probably the best tool for serial assessment in complicated pancreatitis.

ENDOSCOPIC RETROGRADE CHOLANGIOPANCREA-
TOGRAPHY (ERCP) (Figure 27)

The method is described in Chapter 1. Depending upon the circumstances an attempt may be made to outline only the pancreatic duct, or the biliary system as well.

Interpretation

It has been shown that clinical information improves the diagnostic accuracy of pancreatogram reporting, and should always be fully supplied.

Normal

The pancreatic duct passes obliquely cranially from the ampulla and then is roughly transverse. The diameter decreases smoothly and maximal figures are 6.5 mm in the head to 3 mm in the tail. The side ducts are variably filled. There is a wide variation in ductal anatomy. In addition, the examination is complicated by, and may be unsatisfactory in, the annular or malfused pancreas. In elderly patients the duct system may widen up to 10 mm, and ductular ectasia and narrowing can occur without definite pathological significance.

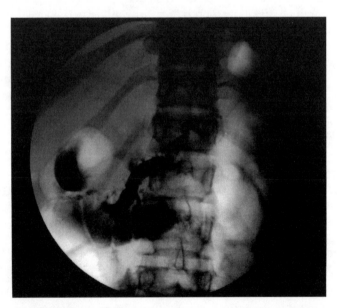

Figure 27 Endoscopic retrograde cholangiopancreatography (ERCP). Dilated pancreatic duct in familial pancreatitis

Chronic pancreatitis

The main duct becomes dilated and tortuous. It may show strictures or contain filling defects. The earliest changes occur in the duct branches, which show variation in calibre and frank dilatation, but these are difficult to detect. In advanced and calculous pancreatitis there may be complete obstruction to the proximal flow of contrast. Pancreatic fistulas can sometimes be seen. ERCP in *acute pancreatitis* will usually demonstrate a *pseudocyst* when it occurs, but needs to be performed cautiously. The main reason for ERCP in this circumstance is identification and treatment of choledocholithiasis.

Pancreatic carcinoma

Abnormalities of the duct system such as obstruction or stenosis occur in 65–80% of patients and the diagnostic rate is highest in the group amenable to surgical removal. The collection of pure pancreatic juice for cytology at the time of ERCP improves the diagnostic rate to 92%.

Indications

(1) Evaluation of chronic and acute relapsing pancreatitis, especially detection of pancreatic ductal abnormalities or biliary calculi requiring surgical treatment.
(2) Differential diagnosis of chronic pancreatitis and carcinoma.
(3) Collection of pure pancreatic juice.
(4) Extraction of bile duct stones.
(5) Position of biliary and pancreatic stents.

COMPUTED TOMOGRAPHY (CT) (Figure 28)

CT scanning can diagnose some pancreatic lesions missed by ultrasonography. The main indication is probably to investigate the patient where other tests have failed, unless the procedure is readily available. Serial CT scanning is especially useful in acute pancreatitis.

Dilute oral barium or iodine contrast media and i.v. iodine contrast media may be helpful in delineating adjacent bowel and blood vessels respectively. Obesity may actually improve results by provision of greater tissue contrast.

OTHER RADIOLOGY

Chest X-ray

This is helpful in the diagnosis of fibrocystic disease of the pancreas when there is evidence of chronic chest infection. In acute pancreatitis basal atelectasis or a pleural effusion (often left-sided) may be present.

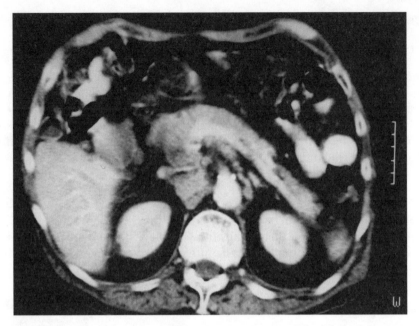

Figure 28 Computed tomography (CT). Carcinoma of the head of the pancreas

Straight abdominal radiograph

The plain radiograph of the abdomen is helpful in acute pancreatitis. An isolated distended loop of jejunum in the upper abdomen, the 'sentinel loop', may be demonstrated or there may be absence of gas in the transverse colon, the 'colon cut-off' sign. The pancreas may be seen to be calcified and stones may be present in the duct. There may be diffuse abdominal calcification following the fat necrosis that occurs in acute pancreatic inflammation.

Barium meal

Helpful signs of pancreatic disease are pressure deformities and displacement of the stomach and duodenum. Expanding pancreatic lesions enlarge the retrogastric space and deform the posterior wall of the stomach. The indentation is smooth in the case of pseudocysts of the pancreas. In cancer the enlargement is usually slight and any infiltration of the stomach results in a rigid appearance. Changes in the gastric antrum are also seen. The duodenum may be enlarged and there may be depression of the ligament of Treitz. Pressure on the medial wall of the duodenum will give the inverted-3 sign of Frostberg which is an indication of a pancreatic mass and does not differentiate cancer from inflammation. Pressure on the lateral aspect of the duodenum with rigidity and compression may occur in pancreatic cancer.

Magnetic resonance imaging

This is probably equivalent to CT scanning but not superior, especially if modern spiral CT scans are performed.

LAPAROSCOPY (peritoneoscopy)

This procedure is described in Chapter 15.

An infragastric method has been devised for diagnosis and staging pancreatic cancer. Direct visualisation permits biopsy or aspiration for cytology and avoids the hazards of laparotomy.

HISTOLOGY AND CYTOLOGY

Guided biopsy with an automatically fired needle is a technique which yields tissue samples and histology is definitely better than cytology where it is possible.

Material for cytology may be obtained by several methods:

(1)   Aspiration of the pancreas by direct puncture at laparotomy or laparoscopy using a standard 21-gauge needle;
(2)   A guided percutaneous puncture with a Chiba needle;
(3)   Collection of pancreatic juice during ERCP or duodenal intubation for the testing of pancreatic function.

At least four smears are made onto slides, which are fixed at once in 95% alcohol and stained. Positive results are obtained in at least 75% of pancreatic cancer patients, while false-positive results are rare.

FLUORESCEIN DILAURATE TEST (Pancreolauryl test) (Figure 29)

The goal of satisfactory tests of pancreatic secretion without the requirement for the need for intubation or handling stools has been reached. Methods are based on the pancreatic enzyme activity on bentiromide, fluoroscein dilaurate and triolein. None of these tests diagnose or exclude pancreatic carcinoma. Bentiromide was also used as a substrate, but is currently unavailable in Britain.

The test is a 2–3-day procedure. The fasting patient is given two blue capsules of fluorescein dilaurate (0.5 mmol) with a standard breakfast including at least 500 ml fluid. A further litre of fluid should be taken 3–5 h later, then normal feeding is resumed. Urine is collected for 10 h and after hydrolysis of a 0.5 ml aliquot with 4.5 ml 0.1 mol/l NaOH, the sample is incubated for 10 min at 65–70 °C, cooled and centrifuged. The supernatant is compared with a water standard by fluorimetry at 492 nm and the percentage dye excreted calculated from the 10-h volume of urine.

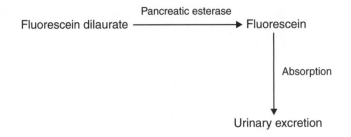

Figure 29 Fluorescein dilaurate test (pancreolauryl test)

On the second day after this test the procedure is repeated with one red capsule containing 0.5 mmol fluorescein sodium. The test is then conducted as before.

The ratio of dye excretion after fluorescein dilaurate and after fluorescein sodium should be greater than 0.3. In pancreatic insufficiency the value will be 0.2 or less. Values from 0.2 to 0.3 are equivocal and the test should be repeated.

The fluorescein dilaurate test can be used in children, where radioactivity should be avoided.

Triolein tests

It is also possible to perform a standard ^{14}C-triolein breath test and then repeat it with supplementary pancreatic enzymes, which will normalise breath $^{14}CO_2$ excretion.

This procedure has theoretical attractions, though is not yet standard.

ORAL GLUCOSE TOLERANCE TEST

This test is described in Chapter 5.

An elevated blood sugar concentration and glycosuria occurs in 15% of patients with *acute pancreatitis*. In *chronic pancreatitis* some abnormality of glucose tolerance occurs in 70% of patients. Glucose tolerance is invariably abnormal in the presence of *pancreatic steatorrhoea*. The test is frequently abnormal when there is derangement of the pancreatic exocrine function tests. Occasionally an abnormal glucose tolerance test is the only manifestation of pancreatic disease. Some abnormality of glucose metabolism has been demonstrated in 20–30% of patients with *pancreatic cancer*. It is thought to have an endocrine basis more complex than simple destruction of the beta cells of the islets.

An *intravenous test* is used to avoid difficulties arising from defective glucose absorption. Such a test is generally unnecessary, because glucose absorption is usually normal in pancreatic disease even when steatorrhoea is present. Occasionally the i.v. test is undertaken to test for diabetes mellitus in patients with coeliac disease or after partial gastrectomy.

DIGESTIVE ENZYMES OUTSIDE THE GUT

At least a dozen digestive enzymes are formed by the pancreas. Not all of them are readily measured in the serum and only three – amylase, trypsin and lipase – have been studied clinically to any extent.

Serum amylase

The units of amylase activity vary according to the method. The methods are potentially less accurate when there is hyperglycaemia and in the presence of jaundice. Lipaemia interferes with the assay, which should be performed only after dilution of the serum by 5–100 times until further dilution produces no more apparent increase in levels.

Interpretation

Characteristically there is elevation of serum amylase concentration in *acute pancreatitis*. The rise starts within 2–12 h of the inflammation, is maximally elevated by the second to fourth day and falls to normal values within 3–6 days. There is no single blood level which is diagnostic for pancreatitis, but an increase five times the upper limit of normal is regarded as diagnostic of acute pancreatitis and levels over twice normal are suggestive. It is not possible to predict the extent of the pancreatic damage from the serum levels. A fall in serum level does not necessarily indicate any improvement in the disease because it may be the consequence of severe destruction of acinar tissue.

There are a number of *extra-hepatic* causes of an elevated serum amylase level including perforated peptic ulcer, small bowel obstruction, peritonitis, viral hepatitis, ectopic pregnancy, inflammation of the salivary glands, and uraemia, but they seldom cause a five-fold elevation. Drugs such as morphine and codeine which produce spasm of the sphincter of Oddi may cause a rise in the serum amylase concentration. Therefore, it is always advisable to stop these drugs for at least 24 h before estimating serum amylase. In all these situations the rise in serum amylase concentration is seldom more than 3–4 times the normal value.

The serum amylase concentration usually returns to normal within a week and persistent elevation generally implies the development of a *pancreatic pseudocyst*. Less common causes of a prolonged elevation of the serum amylase are persistent pancreatitis, partial pancreatic duct obstruction and renal failure.

Macroamylasaemia is a rare cause of raised levels in which there is binding of the amylase to an abnormal globulin with the formation of a macro-molecular complex which is too large to be excreted via the kidneys. This unusual cause is suggested when there is an elevated serum amylase concentration in association with normal or reduced urinary concentrations of the enzyme.

Serum amylase increases usually do not occur in chronic pancreatitis or pancreatic cancer, and if there is elevation it is of a modest degree only. Isoenzyme analysis may be useful to determine the origin of amylase, as in pancreatic insufficiency.

Urinary amylase

Normally amylase is cleared by the kidneys and there is a two- to three-fold rise in acute pancreatitis. The excretion of amylase maybe used as an index of pancreatic amylase released into the blood.

The test is usually performed on a 24-h sample of urine collected into a bottle containing toluene. An increased urinary excretion of enzyme occurs in *acute pancreatitis.* Low values are recorded when there is associated renal failure. An estimation can be performed on a single urine sample in an emergency, but this is inaccurate because enzyme values vary according to the degree of concentration of the sample. Urinary amylase has been expressed as the amount excreted per unit of time in an attempt to increase the accuracy of urinary amylase as a diagnostic test. The hourly excretion rate of the enzyme may be abnormal when the serum enzyme levels are normal.

The urinary amylase concentration falls rapidly although it may take longer than the serum levels to return to normal, and may occasionally remain elevated for 1–2 weeks. The urine analysis may, therefore, be used to diagnose acute pancreatitis at a late stage. The test is of no value in the diagnosis of chronic pancreatic disease.

In an attempt to correct for the hyperamylasaemia of renal failure and for the frequent association of renal impairment with acute pancreatitis, the amylase : creatinine clearance ratio has been proposed. This is based on simultaneous estimation in the serum and urine of both amylase and creatinine. It has not proved as helpful as was originally hoped and is not recommended.

Amylase in other fluids

It is often of value to estimate the amylase activity in ascitic and pleural fluid. High values suggest the presence of acute pancreatitis. The elevation may be as high as blood levels and may persist for 2–3 days longer than in serum. This is sometimes of diagnostic value.

OTHER BLOOD TESTS

Serum calcium

Normal levels are 2.15–2.65 mmol/l when serum albumin is 40 g/dl. A correction can be made for reduced albumin levels by multiplying the number of g/l under 40 g/l by 0.02, and adding the results to the estimated value. Thus, an apparent serum calcium of 2.09 mmol/l with an albumin of 31 g/l corrects to 2.27 mmol/l. A similar correction can be made for elevated serum albumin levels by multiplying the number of g/l over 40 g/l by 0.02 and subtracting the result from the apparent serum calcium.

The serum calcium level is commonly reduced during an attack of acute pancreatitis. It is important to correct values for serum albumin levels, which are often also markedly reduced. The maximum fall in serum calcium is seen 1–2 days after the onset of the attack of pancreatitis. A normal or elevated serum calcium level in the presence of severe pancreatic inflammation should raise the suspicion of associated hyperparathyroidism.

Serum bilirubin

The serum bilirubin may be elevated during an attack of acute pancreatitis. The presence of an elevated value in a patient with recurrent or chronic pancreatitis should always raise the suspicion of pancreatic cancer, though it is not pathognomonic.

Serum alkaline phosphatase

An elevation of serum alkaline phosphatase and gamma-glutamyl transferase (gamma GT) may be found when there is duct obstruction in pancreatic cancer. Raised levels also occur in liver metastases. The association of bone disease with pancreatic dysfunction may be responsible for raised alkaline phosphatase values and this occurs when there is chronic pancreatic insufficiency and steatorrhoea, or hyperparathyroidism and pancreatitis.

Blood gases

In acute pancreatitis there are frequently various disturbances of pulmonary function, and reduction in the arterial oxygen tension (PaO_2) is one of the most constant findings in the condition.

STOOL EXAMINATION

Macroscopic and microscopic examination

In pancreatic insufficiency the stool may appear normal or it may show obvious steatorrhoea by being pale, bulky and offensive.

The stool can be examined for fat droplets and meat fibres. Normally not more than one or two partially-digested meat fibres are seen in a high-power field. The fibres are free from striations and have rounded ends but no nuclei. In pancreatic insufficiency there may be an increase in the number of meat fibres and they are partially digested with striations, irregular ends and nuclei.

Gallstones can be found in the stools of patients with gallstone pancreatitis.

Steatorrhoea

Steatorrhoea may occur during an episode of acute pancreatitis, the stool fat output frequently returning to normal once the inflammation has subsided. Excess fat in the stool may be a prominent feature of chronic pancreatitis and is found in up to 50% of patients. Steatorrhoea is seldom the sole manifestation of pancreatic disease. Fat maldigestion is even less common in pancreatic cancer, occurring in under 20% of patients. It is most likely to occur in cancer of the head of the pancreas.

Stool trypsin and chymotrypsin

Faecal chymotrypsin measurement in adults is a less sensitive test for pancreatic insufficiency than duodenal drainage after pancreatic stimulation. By contrast, in children the test can be very reliable as an index of pancreatic function. Analysis of a 3-day stool collection gives values of 2 mg chymotrypsin/kg body weight or less in cystic fibrosis with steatorrhoea, compared with normal values of 3 mg/kg.

SWEAT ELECTROLYTES

The measurement of the sweat electrolyte concentration is an important investigation in the child with steatorrhoea and malabsorption. Children with fibrocystic disease of the pancreas (mucoviscidosis) have a raised concentration of sodium chloride in the sweat. This fundamental abnormality is present regardless of pancreatic function. The sweat electrolyte excretion is not abnormal in other varieties of pancreatic disease or malabsorption. Pilocarpine iontophoresis is the recommended technique for measuring the sweat electrolyte concentration, but similar results to this test are obtained using methacholine chloride stimulation.

Pilocarpine iontophoresis

Method

Sweat is collected at room temperature from the flexor aspects of either forearm. A direct current source is used. The positive electrode is filled with 0.5% aqueous pilocarpine nitrate solution and the negative with 1% aqueous sodium nitrate solution. The surface of the positive electrode is covered with a circle of ashless filter paper saturated with pilocarpine nitrate solution and the negative electrode with a gauze saturated in the sodium nitrate solution. This is to prevent stinging. A rubber strap holds the positive electrode in place at the midpoint of the flexor surface, and the negative electrode on the extensor surface of the forearm. Circular electrodes are used with a 3 cm diameter.

A current of 1.5 mA is passed for 5 min. The electrolytes are removed and 5 min later the area covered by the positive electrode is washed with distilled water and covered with a circle of Whatman No. 40 ashless filter paper of known weight. The paper is carefully handled with forceps. It is covered with plastic film and the sweat collected for 25–35 min. The paper is removed, weighed, placed in a flask and the electrolytes eluted in 10 ml distilled water. The sodium and chloride concentrations are measured by routine methods.

Interpretation

In *normal infants* the mean sweat sodium is 24 mmol/l and chloride 19 mmol/l. In *cystic fibrosis* the mean concentrations are 110 and 117 mmol/l respectively, and values greater than 70 mmol/l establish the diagnosis. Sweat chloride is the more reliable index.

After the first month of life the sweat sodium and chloride concentrations drop and are low by the end of the first year. Thereafter sweat electrolyte concentrations increase with age.

In *adults* the separation of cystic fibrosis from normal is much less satisfactory, but values of sweat electrolytes over 90 mmol/l are suggestive in a single test, or over 70 mmol/l in each of two tests.

Adult females have lower sweat sodium concentrations than males.

Skin chloride assay

This employs the principle of measuring the chloride content of sweat directly on the skin. First the skin-chloride electrode is calibrated. A pilocarpine-impregnated pad is applied to a well-washed and dried area of the forearm. Current is passed for 5 min, the pad is removed and the area is washed and dried again.

The area is then covered with plastic film and the presence of sweating is observed. Failure to detect sweating invalidates the test.

The direct-reading skin-chloride electrode is placed on the skin immediately the film is removed, taking care that good contact is made without trapping air. The chloride concentration is then read directly, and high levels are seen in cystic fibrosis.

The sweat tests are not infallible and reproducibility can be poor; it is important that they are interpreted with regard to clinical features. Screening of neonatal blood for immunoreactive trypsin, detection of serum cystic fibrosis protein, estimation of salivary and nail-clipping electrolytes, and screening meconium for albumin have all been proposed for the diagnosis of cystic fibrosis.

GENE PROBES IN CYSTIC FIBROSIS

The description of the mutated gene on chromosome 7 (CFTR) has allowed the identification of affected individuals by chorionic villus sampling in the womb, and could have a role in children and adults too.

GUT ENDOCRINOLOGY

Many hormones and candidate hormones have been identified in the gastrointestinal tract since the original description of secretin in 1902. Peptides with a known physiological role are secretin, gastrin, cholecystokinin-pancreozymin and glucagon. There are many others including vasoactive intestinal peptide (VIP), gastric inhibitory peptide (GIP), motilin, bombesin, substance P, pancreatic polypeptide (PP) and the potent secretion-inhibitor somatostatin. More recently the endorphins and the prostaglandins have been postulated to have important functions. Because the physiological role of most of the hormones is doubtful, measuring levels in tissue and serum does not usually assist in diagnosis, with the important exception of the endocrine tumours or hyperplasias which are frequently located in the pancreatic islets. The two most common of these are insulinomas and gastrinomas (causing the Zollinger–Ellison syndrome). Well recognised but rare are glucagonomas, and vipomas (causing the watery diarrhoea/hypokalaemia/achlorhydria or Verner–Morrison syndrome from overproduction of vasoactive intestinal peptide).

Insulinoma

This is a notoriously difficult tumour to diagnose. Symptoms can include periodic dizziness and blackouts, epileptic fits and psychiatric disturbances. It is necessary to demonstrate both that the symptoms are due to hypoglycaemia and that the hypoglycaemia is the consequence of an insulin-secreting tumour of the beta cells of the pancreatic islets.

The diagnosis depends on the demonstration of hypoglycaemia with appropriately high insulin levels.

Prolonged starvation

The patient is fasted for up to 72 h but allowed to drink water. This induces hypoglycaemia and produces symptoms which are relieved by rapid intravenous glucose administration. The test is carried out in the hospital with careful supervision of the patient. Blood sugar samples are taken at regular intervals (at least twice daily) and also if symptoms develop. Two-thirds of patients with insulinomas develop symptoms within 24 h and virtually all do so within 48 h; the demonstrations of a blood glucose of less than 1.7 mmol/l when there are symptoms is especially useful.

At the times of blood sugar estimation, samples of serum are taken and stored frozen. If the patient develops hypoglycaemia then these are analysed for immunoreactive insulin. A positive diagnosis is made by the finding of a ratio of:

$$\frac{\text{Immunoreactive insulin (microunits / ml)}}{\text{Blood glucose (mmol / l)}}$$

of 0.3 or greater.

Glucagon test

Glucagon 1 mg is injected intravenously and venous blood samples are taken at 0, 10, 20, 30, 45, 60, 90, 120, 150 and 180 min. An assay is made for glucose and insulin. In normal subjects the blood sugar rises and falls much as in an oral glucose tolerance test.

When an insulinoma is present the period of raised blood sugar levels is shorter and is followed by an abrupt and pronounced fall in blood sugar, even to hypoglycaemic levels. Plasma insulin levels are greater than 100 microunits/ml after 10 min. This is in many respects the safest of the provocative tests.

The test can be performed by injection 1 mg glucagon intramuscularly and testing the capillary blood.

Gastrinoma (Zollinger–Ellison syndrome)

Clinical features include multiple unusually-sited and recurrent peptic ulcers, diarrhoea and steatorrhoea, diabetes mellitus and occasional skin rashes. The best screening test is the measurement of the ratio of basal acid output to peak acid output, which is usually in excess of 60%. Fasting serum gastrin levels, usually well over 50 μmol/l confirm the diagnosis. A secretin provocation test can be helpful in doubtful cases, when intravenous injection of secretin 1 unit/kg provokes a rapid rise in serum gastrin levels.

Barium radiology may be helpful, showing coarse gastric folds, multiple ulcers and a dilated and oedematous duodenum. Selective arteriography may localise a pancreatic islet tumour, though frequently undetectable diffuse gastrin-cell hyperplasia occurs.

Obscure diarrhoea

In intractable diarrhoeas which are undiagnosable despite exhaustive investigation, the estimation of a panel for serum hormones such as insulin, gastrin, calcitonin, vasoactive intestinal peptide and pancreatic polypeptide may occasionally be rewarding. Factitious diarrhoea should be borne in mind. It is more common in medical personnel, and may be diagnosed from the clinical picture or from an examination of the bedside locker or medicine chest. Some proprietary laxatives contain phenolphthalein, which can be demonstrated in the stool by dropwise addition of 0.1 mol/l sodium hydroxide. In a positive reaction a purple colour develops in the stool.

PANCREATIC CANCER

The difficulty of diagnosing exocrine pancreatic cancer has stimulated the development of a host of tumour markers such as CEA, pancreatic oncofetal antigen and monoclonal antibody-based tests for carbohydrate antigens such as CA19-9. None is entirely specific or satisfactory, but they may play a role in combination with other tests and in serial monitoring of progress in individuals.

Normally CA19-9 should be up to 37 kU/l, CA125 up to 35 kU/l and CA195 up to 20 kU/l. Values of greater than 1000 kU/l indicate poorer prognosis. Serum testosterone is characteristically low.

11

Liver Biochemistry

Blood tests remain the first investigations in the assessment of liver dysfunction. None of the tests is entirely specific, and interpretation usually depends on examination of a constellation of results, together with the clinical presentation. There is no true 'liver function' test, but merely abnormal serum biochemistry which could be explained by liver disease.

SERUM BILIRUBIN

Although harmless in adults, the visible nature of hyperbilirubinaemia makes this an obvious marker of liver disease. Jaundice may, however, result from three distinct processes:

(1) *Haemolysis.* There is excess production of unconjugated bilirubin due to red cell destruction. The jaundice is usually independent of hepatobiliary disease, unless there is secondary hypersplenism.
(2) *Hepatocellular damage.* There is a failure of conjugation of bilirubin. Unconjugated bilirubin accumulates in the bloodstream. There is also some reduction in excretory capacity for conjugated bilirubin which may also contribute to raised levels.
(3) *Cholestasis.* Conjugated bilirubin is not excreted because of dysfunction of the bile secretory mechanism at the bile canaliculus (*intrahepatic cholestasis)* or because of an *extrahepatic obstruction.*

These causes can be inter-related: for example, cirrhosis with some liver cell necrosis may be accompanied by intrahepatic cholestasis and haemolysis.

Patients with *carotenaemia* from excess dietary carotene associated with hypothyroidism may also develop yellow skin, but unlike hyperbilirubinaemia there is no conjunctival colouring.

Jaundice is usually detectable when serum bilirubin rises above 50 µmol/l and can often be seen at lower levels. Variable tissue levels in fluctuating jaundice may mean that skin and conjunctival appearances do not correlate.

Laboratory measurements of serum bilirubin are based on a diazo colour reaction which forms the purple azobilirubin. Conjugated (direct) bilirubin reacts quickly.

Unconjugated (indirect) bilirubin reacts slowly and requires the addition of alcohol for complete reaction. There are considerable technical problems associated with fractionation of bilirubin; at very low levels of total bilirubin, as well as when there is considerable elevation, the ratio of conjugated : un-conjugated bilirubin is unreliable.

Interpretation

The normal serum bilirubin is less than 17 µmol/l in woman and less than 23 µmol in men. Half or less is conjugated. In *haemolysis* there is increase in unconjugated bilirubin, and unless there is associated liver disease the con-jugated bilirubin level remains low.

In *cholestasis* ('obstructive' jaundice, either intra- or extrahepatic) the conjugated bilirubin is characteristically raised. Prolonged cholestasis may, however, lead to liver failure, and there may also be some elevation of unconjugated bilirubin.

In *hepatocellular damage* both fractions of bilirubin are raised, although usually unconjugated bilirubin predominates. Occasionally the rise is due entirely to conjugated bilirubin.

For serial monitoring of the progress of liver disease, total bilirubin meas-urement is adequate.

URINE UROBILINOGEN

Urobilinogens are formed from bilirubin by bacterial action in the intestine. Most are excreted in the faeces but some are absorbed and excreted in the urine. The excretion is maximal between 2 and 4 pm, and is enhanced by an alkaline urine. On exposure to air the urobilinogen is oxidised to urobilin, which darkens the urine.

Interpretation

Normal urine gives either no colour reaction or only a faint red colour which is intensified by gentle heating. A distinctly red colour at room temperature is indicative of increased amounts of urobilinogen. A rough quantitation can be made by serial dilutions of the coloured urine to find the greatest dilution which shows a pink colour. Normal urine shows no colour when diluted more than 1 : 20.

A false-negative result may be given if urine is tested after it has been standing for some time at room temperature. Antibiotic therapy may result in urobilinogen being absent from the urine because of the destruction of the intestinal bacteria. The test is a useful method for distinguishing between obstructive jaundice on the one hand and hepatocellular and haemolytic jaundice on the other. In the former there is no urobilinogen in the urine whereas in the latter conditions urobilirubinogenuria may be present. A positive result can be found in many febrile patients.

Testing for urine urobilinogen has been simplified by the introduction of a dipstick test which provides a semi-quantitative record.

Table 4 Changes in bile pigment metabolism associated with the various types of jaundice

Disease	Stool appearance	Urine			Blood	
		Urobilinogen	Bilirubin	Appearance	Conjugated bilirubin	Unconjugated bilirubin
Haemolytic jaundice	Normal	Increased	Absent	Normal	Normal	Increased
Cholestatic jaundice	Pale	Absent	Present	Dark	Increased	Normal or increased
Hepatocellular jaundice	Normal	Variable (high, low, normal)	Present	Normal	Increased	Increased

In the presence of cholestasis the stools become pale because of absence of bile pigment in the intestine. This does not occur in haemolysis or hepato-cellular jaundice.

SERUM ENZYMES

A number of intracellular enzymes appear in the serum when liver cells are damaged. Different patterns of elevation suggest different disorders, but none is pathognomonic. The mechanism of elevated serum levels is leakage from the cells linked with the increased synthesis of enzymes because of induction prior to necrosis.

Transaminases

Both aspartate aminotransferase, EC2.6.1.1 (AST, SGOT) and alanine amino-transferase, EC 2.6.1.2 (ALT, SGPT) are elevated in hepatocellular damage. ALT is slightly more specific to the liver.

The normal serum AST concentration is up to 40 IU/l and the normal ALT up to 50 IU/l. Marked elevations in concentration occur in acute hepatitis and hepatic necrosis, and levels of 150–1000 IU/l are fairly common. Lesser elevation, usually below 150 IU/l, are recorded in infectious mononucleosis, drug cholestasis, metastatic cancer of the liver, cirrhosis and extrahepatic obstruction. Occasionally marked elevations of ALT + AST concentration are found in extrahepatic obstruction. On the other hand, patients may die from acute hepatitis without an elevation in serum enzyme concentrations. Thus, transaminase levels have their limitations in the diagnosis of liver disease and jaundice. The serum transaminase concentration may be the only biochemi-cal abnormality present in patients with hepatitis and this estimation has been used in epidemiological screening studies.

ALT + AST are present in many of the body cells and elevated serum levels accompany bowel necrosis, pancreatitis, myocardial infarction and other disorders. These conditions are usually readily distinguished from liver disease and, therefore, the source of an elevated level is seldom a problem when investigating a patient with liver disease. In liver disease where the AST is greater than twice the ALT level, alcohol is likely to be the cause.

Alkaline phosphatase

The serum alkaline phosphatase (EC3.1.3.1) originates from the liver, bones, intestines and placenta. The upper limit of normal is 100 IU/l. Children and adolescents normally have increased serum alkaline phosphatase concentration levels because of bone growth.

The serum alkaline phosphatase is a relatively insensitive test of hepatocellular function. The concentration is raised in the presence of intra- or extrahepatic biliary obstruction. A normal value excludes mechanical obstruction of the bile ducts with 95% confidence. A more moderate increase in enzyme levels is found in acute hepatitis and cirrhosis. High levels in a patient with cirrhosis suggest the presence of either co-existent biliary tract disease or hepatoma. Elevated concentrations in the absence of jaundice may be found in primary and secondary liver tumours, primary biliary cirrhosis, lesions of the bile duct, abscesses, granulomas and amyloidosis. While this enzyme is of help for determining whether there is obstruction to the outflow of bile, or irritation of the biliary epithelium, it is of no value in deciding the site of the lesion.

Elevated serum concentrations are found in bone disorders in which there is increased osteoblastic activity such as Paget's disease, osteogenic secondary deposits, osteomalacia and rickets. The identification and differentiation of the serum alkaline phosphatase isoenzymes is technically difficult. The electrophoretic characteristics of the alkaline phosphatases of skeletal and hepatic origin are similar, but they can be separated on polyacrylamide gel.

Gamma-glutamyl transferase (gamma-GT)

The test for this enzyme (EC 2.3.2.2) is the most sensitive widely available test of disordered hepatobiliary function. Unfortunately it is very non-specific, and the level can be raised in pancreatic and renal disease, as well as by drug induction of liver enzymes.

Normal values are up to 50 IU/l. It is particularly useful in the diagnosis of alcoholic liver disease. Elevated levels are characteristic of biliary disease and all the disorders which raise hepatic alkaline phosphatase levels. Since gamma-GT levels are not raised in bone disease, their estimation may help to elucidate the cause of elevated alkaline phosphatase levels.

Table 5 Patterns of abnormal 'liver function' tests

	Gilbert's syndrome	Haemolysis	Anticonvulsant therapy	Early primary biliary cirrhosis
Bilirubin	↑ (unconjugated)	↑↑	N	N
Alkaline phosphatase (AP)	N	N	↑	↑↑
Gamma-glutamyl transferase (gamma-GT)	N	N	↑	↑↑
Alanine amino-transferase (ALT SGPT)	N	N	N	N or ↑
Albumin	N	N	N	N
Immuno-globulins (Ig)	N	N	N	↑↑

	Hepatitis (viral, alcoholic, drug, autoimmune)	Biliary obstruction	Liver metastases	Alcoholic liver disease	Cirrhosis
Bilirubin	↑	↑↑↑	N or ↑	N or ↑	N or ↑
AP	↑	↑↑↑	↑↑↑	↑	N
Gamma-GT	↑	↑↑↑	↑↑↑	↑↑↑	N
ALT, SGPT	↑↑↑↑	↑	N	N or ↑ or ↑↑	N
Albumin	N or ↓	N	N	N or ↓	↓
Ig	↑or↑↑or↑↑↑	N	N	N	N or ↑

PROTEINS

Albumin

Albumin is synthesised in the liver. Normal serum values are 35–50 g/l and can be affected by a number of factors. There are elevated values in dehydration and low levels in fluid retention. Serum albumin may fall because of increased loss, especially in nephrotic syndrome or in protein-losing enteropathy. Reduced synthesis may occur in severe malnutrition, such as kwashiorkor, where there are insufficient dietary essential amino acids. Congenitally low levels of albumin occur in α_1-antitrypsin deficiency, which can cause hepatitis, cirrhosis and emphysema.

The level of serum albumin is helpful in assessing the severity of liver cell failure as well as in predicting the likely cause of ascites. It should always be available to assist the interpretation of serum calcium levels.

Globulins

Many laboratories report globulin levels as the difference between serum total protein and serum albumin. This is only of very limited usefulness. Much more information is gained by the performance of immunoglobulin electrophoresis or by quantitation of serum immunoglobulins.

Immunoglobulins

The normal values for the major immunoglobulins are:

IgG	7–18 g/l
IgA	0.5–4.5 g/l
IgM	0.3–2.5 g/l

The pattern of immunoglobulins is rarely diagnostic and may be affected by diseases which do not involve the gastrointestinal system. There is often considerable overlap in abnormal levels between diseases.

- *IgG* levels are elevated in acute infections including viral hepatitis, and also in chronic autoimmune hepatitis; they are reduced in hypogammaglobulinaemia.

- *IgM* levels are elevated in primary biliary cirrhosis and macroglobulinaemia.

- *IgA* levels may be high in cirrhosis. They are usually normal in coeliac disease, but about 1 in 70 patients have low levels. If they are elevated in a patient with coeliac disease then the presence of a lymphoma should be suspected.

- Measurement of *IgE* levels (normal up to 100 u/l) may prove of value in appraisal of allergic symptoms.

Electrophoresis

Electrophoresis may provide further information. In myeloma there is a distinct monoclonal band in the γ-globulins which accounts for the elevated IgG levels. A diffuse increase in γ-globulins is seen in viral hepatitis and may also occur in cirrhosis. By contrast, an increase in α_2- and β-globulins is more characteristic of cholestasis. α_1-Globulin is markedly reduced or absent in α_1-antitrypsin deficiency and in neonatal hepatitis.

COAGULATION TESTS

Multiple coagulation defects are not uncommon in patients with acute and chronic liver disease. Combined deficiencies of factors II (prothrombin), V, VII and X contribute to an abnormally prolonged prothrombin time. Thus the determination of the one-stage prothrombin time is a useful simple test of liver function. Because vitamin K is a co-factor of hepatic prothrombin synthesis there may be a prolonged prothrombin time in cholestatic jaundice from any cause. The ability of parenteral vitamin K (10 mg vitamin K_1 given i.v./i.m. for 3 days) to convert the prothrombin time to normal values has been used as a diagnostic test of the aetiology of jaundice. Patients with extrahepatic biliary obstruction respond to vitamin K_1 injections, but in severe hepatocellular disease the prothrombin time remains unchanged. This is not a reliable diagnostic test.

Other haematological defects which may be found in liver disease include deficiencies of factors IX (plasma thromboplastin component), XI (plasma thromboplastin antecedent) and platelets.

Liver disease may be accompanied by diffuse intravascular coagulation in which fibrin degradation products appear in the serum (>40 mg/l), the platelet count falls sharply and there is evidence of haemolysis.

LIPIDS

Serum total cholesterol rises in both intra- and extrahepatic cholestasis. This results from the presence of an abnormal lipoprotein (LPX) in the serum which is not a risk factor for heart disease. Very low levels of high-density lipoprotein (HDL) cholesterol are characteristic of cholestasis; the lower limit of normal is about 1 mmol/l.

The presence of altered or abnormal lipoprotein components can be associated with many liver diseases. Raised levels of cholesterol, triglycerides, low-density (LDL) and very low-density (VLDL) lipoprotein in various combinations is seen. This may be important since markedly elevated serum triglycerides (i.e. >10 mmol/l) cause turbidity and interfere with most other biochemical measurements. Alcoholism is the most common cause of secondary hyperlipidaemia, and may itself cause cirrhosis and pancreatitis.

OTHERS

Fluid-electrolyte disturbances including secondary aldosteronism are encountered in liver disease, and *hyponatraemia* (<130 mmol/l) and *hypokalaemia* (<3.5 mmol/l) are common. Although low serum sodium levels are often well tolerated, low serum potassium can potentiate hepatic encephalopathy. *Urea* is synthesised in the liver. Low levels (<3.3 mmol/l) may indicate severe hepatocellular dysfunction but can also reflect dilution with fluid retention. In the presence of associated renal impairment, blood urea may be apparently normal in liver disease, and serum *creatinine* (normal range 45–150 μmol/l) is a better index of renal failure.

Vitamin B_{12} is normally present in liver cells and levels are elevated in metastatic liver disease, liver abscess and hepatitis. Levels also rise in patients on hydroxocobalamin therapy. Plasma *glucose* levels may be informative as both diabetes mellitus and hypoglycaemia occur in liver disease.

ALCOHOLIC LIVER DISEASE

Alcohol is the commonest cause of liver disease. The main hurdle in diagnosis is to suspect the cause and the patient's general demeanour may give clues.

The 'CAGE' questionnaire is a simple four-point system to assess alcohol abuse. A patient who answers 'yes' to all four questions is an alcoholic, and two to three out of four is suspicious.

(1)   Have you ever tried to Cut down alcohol intake?
(2)   Have you ever been Annoyed by criticism of your drinking?
(3)   Have you ever felt Guilty about the amount you drink?
(4)   Do you ever take an 'Eye-opener' – a drink to start the day?

Patients may be teetotal at the time when they are suffering the effects of previous heavy drinking, and an assessment of the amount drunk needs to take into account changing patterns.

Patients are not always honest about excess alcohol intake, and laboratory tests are often valuable in establishing diagnoses. They are not infallible, and all can be normal in severe alcoholic liver disease. In addition, a significant minority of alcohol abusers have liver disease for unconnected reasons.

Measurement of the alcohol level in the blood is extremely useful. If there is any alcohol at all in a morning sample then the patient is probably drinking to excess.

The assessment of long-term heavy drinking is helped by various tests. The most useful are raised gamma-GT levels (over 50 IU/l) and mean corpuscular volumes (over 95 fl). The alkaline phosphatase level may also be raised to a lesser extent, and the platelet count reduced. Chest radiology may reveal old or recent rib fractures in binge drinkers.

TUMOUR ANTIGENS

Alpha-fetoprotein

This may be detected in the serum of patients with hepatoma (primary liver cell carcinoma). In some parts of the world almost all hepatoma patients have detectable levels, although in northern Europe and North America the figure is lower. It is a reliable test if strongly positive, but expression of results semi-quantitatively has shown some weakly positive results of uncertain significance. It may also be detected in ascitic fluid. This test is also positive in pregnant women carrying fetuses with spinal malformations and in neonatal hepatitis. The normal value is up to 10 µg/l, but hepatoma patients commonly have values in 4 figures or more.

Carcinoembryonic and oncofetal antigens

These markers of colonic and pancreatic carcinomas may have a role in monitoring progress of proved disease, such as detecting tumour recurrence and metastasis to the liver and elsewhere. The normal value for CEA is up to 2.5 µg/l.

Tissue antibodies

Circulating antibodies to various tissue components have been described in liver disease. While these antibodies are of great theoretical interest, their detection has variable diagnostic significance.

Perinuclear-anti-neutrophil cytoplasmic antibody (pANCA)

This is a very common finding in primary sclerosing cholangitis (78%) and chronic autoimmune hepatitis (88%). It is less common in primary biliary cirrhosis but is not seen in non-autoimmune liver disease. It does, however, occur in many non-hepatic diseases. Cytosolic ANCA is specific for Wegener's granuloma.

Antimitochondrial antibody (AMA)

These antibodies are found in the sera of 95% of patients with primary biliary cirrhosis. They are rarely present in viral or drug hepatitis. Of great diagnostic value is the finding that these antibodies are rarely present in extrahepatic obstruction and then only in a very low titre. These antibodies provide the most diagnostic help of all the antibody tests.

The M_2 ATPase-associated fraction of mitochondrial antibody is even more specific for primary biliary cirrhosis, and should now be a routine investigation if liver biopsy confirmation is not possible.

Antismooth muscle antibody (SMA)

About one-half of patients with chronic autoimmune hepatitis demonstrate the presence of antibodies reactive with smooth muscle. Positive reactions also occur in 30% of patients with primary biliary cirrhosis, 25% of patients with idiopathic cirrhosis, and 15% with alcoholic liver disease.

The patients with chronic autoimmune hepatitis have high-titre IgG SMA, which is important because 50–80% of patients with viral hepatitis have transient low-titre IgM SMA. There is evidence that the antibody is directed against actin, and the usefulness of measurement of specific *antiactin antibody* is more specific than SMA, but not so readily available.

Antinuclear antibody (ANA)

Antinuclear antibody (or factor) is present in 50% of patients with chronic autoimmune hepatitis, where it is an IgG antibody in high titre (greater than 1 : 80). It also occurs commonly in primary biliary cirrhosis and drug-associated chronic hepatitis. Low titres are of no importance.

The more specific antibody directed against double-stranded DNA is a common accompaniment of all forms of liver disease, and does not assist differential diagnosis.

Liver-kidney microsomal antibody (LKM)

This is found in 'type 2' chronic autoimmune hepatitis where SMA and ANA are both negative.

VIRAL LIVER DISEASE

Viral hepatitis is usually diagnosed on clinical grounds supported by appropriate biochemical tests. Electron microscopy and liver biopsy provide further evidence. It should usually be possible to define the exact organism involved by serum immunology.

Liver biopsy

This is often diagnostic, but is not usually necessary to confirm viral hepatitis. It may be misleading early in the illness. Characteristic changes include cloudy swelling of the cytoplasm ('ground-glass' appearance), with the appearance of eosinophilic cell debris (Councilman bodies) and necrotic nuclei.

Immunofluorescence demonstrates intracellular viral antigens, and viral particles can be seen on electron microscopy.

Hepatitis A

Exposure to this virus (HAV) is widespread, and infections are mild. Antibody to the virus (anti-HAV) in the IgG class is frequently present in serum of healthy individuals with immunity. The appearance of IgG anti-HAV in a patient known to have been previously negative is evidence of recent exposure. Better proof is the detection of anti-HAV in the IgM class, which is transient but always present at the onset of jaundice in HAV infection. It is possible to find 29-mm virus particles in stool by electron microscopy.

Hepatitis B

Acute infection with this virus (HBV) is marked by the appearance in the serum of an antigen associated with the surface protein coat (HB_sAg).

It is usually cleared in a matter of weeks, with a rise in a specific antibody directed against it (HB$_s$Ab or anti-HB$_s$). In 5–10% of patients HB$_s$Ag persists indefinitely. Anti-HB$_s$ is detectable in the serum for long periods and possibly permanently: it only indicates exposure to HBV or surface antigen in vaccine at some time in the past, and is a reliable marker of immunity.

In acute infection with HBV, antigen from the viral core (HB$_c$Ag) may sometimes be found in the serum. Antibody to HB$_c$Ag (HB$_c$Ab or anti-HB$_c$) is much more commonly found, and the presence of anti-HB$_c$Ab of the IgM class in high titre reliably indicates recent infection. Another antibody directed against the intact virion may also be found in serum of currently infected patients, as may viral DNA polymerase and HBV DNA.

There are other useful markers of HBV infection. In an individual who is a chronic carrier of HBsAg, the presence of another antigen from the protein coat (HB$_e$Ag) is an indicator of infectivity. If there is antibody to HB$_e$Ag (HB$_e$Ab or anti-HB$_e$), or if neither HB$_e$Ag nor HB$_e$ Ab are present, the serum is unlikely to be infectious. Electron microscopy of serum will show the 40–44-mm virus, together with the cylindrical and spherical remnants of its protein coat.

Chronic liver disease, including steatosis, persistent hepatitis, or cirrhosis are features of hepatitis B and C.

Hepatitis C

This RNA virus is transmitted parenterally, and many i.v. drug addicts and haemophiliacs are chronically infected.

The initial illness is often mild or unapparent, but serious long-term liver damage may occur anyway. This often requires liver biopsy to document: routine serum biochemistry correlates poorly. The initial test is anti-HCV antibody estimation by ELISA. This may give false-positives so it is useful to confirm infection by back-up radio immuno blot assay (RIBA), which must be positive in at least 2 of the 4 bands to prove the diagnosis. HCV RNA is an indicator of active current infection.

Viral hepatitis prevalence

In Britain hepatitis A is the commonest problem. Acute hepatitis B is decidedly uncommon, and afflicts mainly risk groups like male homosexuals, and i.v. drug addicts. Hepatitis C affects similar groups to hepatitis B and is also said to be the commonest cause of post-transfusion viral hepatitis, although now this seems to be rare because of the screened voluntary donor system. Transfusion and liver transplantation may also spread or reactivate cytomegalovirus, detectable by CMV antibodies. It is also known that transfusion spreads other viruses such as HGV or TTV, whose clinical significance is unclear.

The pattern is quite different in other countries. Hepatitis B virus-associated hepatoma is a common cause of male cancer death world-wide.

Table 6 Viral hepatitis markers and their significance

Finding	Usual significance
Hepatitis A	
IgM anti-HAV	Acute hepatitis A
IgG anti-HAV	Immune to hepatitis A
Hepatitis B	
HBcAg	Acute or chronic hepatitis B carriage
IgM HBcAb	Acute hepatitis B (high titre)
	Chronic hepatitis B (low titre)
IgG HBcAb	Past exposure to hepatitis B
	(with negative HBsAg)
	Chronic hepatitis B
	(with positive HBsAg)
HBsAb	Immune to hepatitis B
HBeAg	Acute hepatitis B. Persistence means
	continued infectious state
HBeAb	Convalescence or non-infectious state
HBV DNA	Continued infection
Hepatitis C	
Anti-HCV ELISA	Acute or chronic infection
HCV RIBA	2–4 band confirms HCV infection
HCV RNA	Continued infection

CONSTITUTIONAL UNCONJUGATED HYPERBILIRUBINAEMIA (Gilbert's syndrome)

Patients with this condition usually have elevated unconjugated and total serum bilirubin levels, or a history of jaundice in the absence of any other symptom or abnormal tests. It is important to make a positive diagnosis in order to allay anxiety about more serious conditions.

Reduced calorie intake test

The patient has blood withdrawn for a total and fractionated serum bilirubin estimation, while taking a normal diet. A diet reduced in energy intake to 1.7 MJ (400 cal) daily is then given for 2 days and further blood samples are taken at 24 and 48 h for bilirubin estimation.

A positive result is a rise in serum bilirubin of 100% or more, with the proviso that the rise must be into the abnormal range and be mainly accounted for by an increase in unconjugated bilirubin. Although the test is specific it does not identify all patients, and furthermore individuals with Gilbert's syndrome may have other hepatobiliary disorders. The test depends on appropriate dietetic advice (the permitted daily food intake is equivalent toa modest breakfast), and if this is not available, putting a patient on water only for 2 days can be used.

HAEMOCHROMATOSIS

This diagnosis should only be made when there is no overt cause for iron overload. A strong family history and the presence of cardiac and endocrine disease are valuable pointers.

Serum iron and iron-binding capacity

Serum iron may fluctuate and is low in many acute and inflammatory diseases.

In haemochromatosis the serum iron is usually raised with a normal iron binding capacity which is 80–100% saturated. Serum ferritin is often over 1000 µg/ml, and correlates well with total body stores.

Iron excretion

A simple test, suitable for out-patients, is the measurement of the iron content in a 24-h urine collection after 0.5 g desferrioxamine intramuscularly. An iron output of greater than 30 µmol (2 mg) indicates iron overload, and in untreated haemochromatosis the excretion is usually over 180 µmol (10 mg) in 24 h.

Liver biopsy

This is essential to prove the diagnosis. Iron deposits stain brown with haematoxylin and eosin, and blue with Perl's reagent. In haemochromatosis iron content is ++ or more on the semi-quantitive 0 – ++++ score, and is in excess of 180 µmol/g (1 g/100 g) dry weight of liver.

Other tests

Excess iron occurs in the reticuloendothelial bone marrow cells and deposits also occur in the skin and gastric mucosa.

Liver iron stores are shown as diffuse sonodense areas on ultrasonography and this can be used to monitor removal by treatment.

Patients are usually diabetic, though glucose tolerance is also often impaired in other forms of cirrhosis. The ECG may show dysrrhythmias and flattened T-waves. Iron absorption is increased (as it is also in porphyria), though this may not be a constant abnormality. Testosterone levels are low and there may be evidence of both adrenal and pituitary failure. The genetic marker HLA-HFE is specific to haemochromatosis, and occurs in most cases.

75% of patients carry HLA A3 (vs. 30% in general population), and affected relatives will often carry similar HLA types to patients.

WILSON'S DISEASE

Wilson's disease (hepatolenticular degeneration) is an autosomal recessive disease in which excessive tissue copper deposits occur. It may show itself as nerve damage (Parkinsonism and mental changes) or as liver disease (cirrhosis). Detection of asymptomatic sufferers is important in preventing progression of the disease. Abnormal hepatic copper deposits have been described in other diseases, such as primary biliary cirrhosis, sclerosing cholangitis and chronic cholestasis.

Serum copper and caeruloplasmin

In normal subjects caeruloplasmin levels are 200–400 mg/l. This copper-binding protein with oxidase activity binds 60–120 µg/100 ml copper in the serum. There is an additional 5–10 µg/100 ml non-caeruloplasmin copper.

In 95% of patients with Wilson's disease the serum caeruloplasmin levels are below 200 mg/l with a serum caeruloplasmin copper under 60 µg/100 ml. Sometimes the non-caeruloplasmin copper increases in Wilson's disease.

A screening test for copper oxidase activity, taken as equivalent to caeruloplasmin, is widely used. The normal range is 0.2–0.7 optical density units.

Urine copper

The normal subject excretes about 30 µg/24 h. In symptomatic Wilson's disease more than 100 µg/24 h is excreted, derived from the non-caeruloplasmin serum copper.

Liver biopsy

Cirrhosis is seen and copper can be stained brown-black with rubeanic acid in 70% alcohol. The copper content of the biopsy is measured. In normals this is 20–50 µg/g dry weight of liver. In Wilson's disease before treatment, liver copper is 250–300 µg/g dry weight. The biopsy needle must be rendered copper-free by washing with 0.5% EDTA and then rising with 5% dextrose.

Kayser–Fleischer rings

These are caused by copper deposits in the cornea. If not obvious to the naked eye they should be sought by slit-lamp examination. They may occur in other causes of copper overload.

ACUTE INTERMITTENT PORPHYRIA

This may present as abdominal pain, neuropathy or coma, but the basic problem is over-activity of the δ-aminolaevulinic acid synthetase in the liver. Liver histology is normal.

It is convenient to perform a simple urine screening test where the diagnosis is suspected, and then proceed to a full biochemical evaluation.

Screening test

Equal volumes of urine and Ehrlich's reagent are mixed in a tube. If the solution goes pink there is either porphobilinogen or urobilinogen present.

Porphobilinogen may be confirmed by adding two volumes of chloroform and shaking thoroughly. On settling, the pink colour should remain in the upper aqueous layer.

By contrast, urobilinogen would colour the lower chloroform layer pink.

Confirmatory tests

A variety of tests can be used to prove the diagnosis:

(1)   Urine will turn port wine colour on standing.
(2)   Urine will contain increased porphobilinogen (normal up to 16 μmol/day)
(3)   Increased urine porphyrin : creatinine ratio (normal up to 42)
(4)   Increased serum protoporphyin (normal 0–900 nmol/l)
(5)   Reduced serum porphobilinogen deaminase (normal 3–54 units)

In *porphyria cutanea tarda* there is commonly alcoholic liver disease or cirrhosis.

There are a whole family of porphyrias, hepatic and erythropoetic, and where they are suspected full evaluation will include examination of urine for increased porphyrins:

normal δ-aminolaevulinic acid	0–40 μmol/day
normal uroporphyrin	0–49 nmol/day
normal coproporphyrin	0–430 nmol/day

and also stool for increased porphyrins:

normal coproporphyrin	0–76 nmol/g dry weight
normal protoporphyrin	0–200 nmol/g dry weight

Porphyria is familial and screening blood relatives is important to identify those at risk and to protect them from precipitating attacks.

12

Liver Biopsy

The histology of the liver is an indispensable aid to diagnosis. It is the only unequivocal way of proving the presence of cirrhosis, and it may also establish the cause of this disease, as in haemochromatosis and hepatolenticular degeneration. It has proved invaluable in the assessment of chronic hepatitis and alcoholic liver disease.

PERCUTANEOUS LIVER BIOPSY

Since the liver is the largest organ in the body and is relatively constant in position, blind percutaneous biopsy is satisfactory in most patients. However, the use of ultrasound or CT guidance improves results in focal lesions and may be safer in parenchymal disease.

Preparation

The nature of the investigation is explained to the patient; it is preferable to obtain written consent. Blood is taken for haemoglobin, prothrombin time and platelet count. If there is any reason to suspect these variables may change then the tests should be repeated on the day of the biopsy.

A biopsy should not normally be performed unless the haemoglobin is over 10 g/100 ml, the platelet count over 100 000/mm^3 and prothrombin time no more than 3 s longer than the control. Liver biopsy should also be avoided in the presence of substantial ascites or when extrahepatic cholestasis seems likely. In anxious patients premedication with diazepam by mouth or i.v. midazolam may be helpful, but routine premedication is not necessary and may interfere with co-operation.

Procedure

The patient is positioned on the examination couch, or better still on the bed or trolley on which they will lie after the procedure. The patient lies supine close to the right edge of the bed. The right hand is placed behind the head which is supported by one pillow. The position of the liver is confirmed by percussion down the right side of the chest and abdomen. The puncture site is the point of maximal dullness between the anterior and mid-axillary lines. This usually lies in the 8th–10th intercostal spaces. The puncture site is positioned just above the appropriate rib, to avoid the vessels and nerves which run just below the ribs.

Occasionally, in case of difficulty, or when a nodule can be palpated, a subcostal puncture may be made; this is a less satisfactory procedure even in the presence of marked liver enlargement.

It is not necessary to wear gowns or masks for this procedure, but the use of surgical gloves for the operator is recommended. A paper sheet placed under the patient prevents any leakage of blood onto the bedding.

The patient is instructed to practise the breath-holding procedure: after a full inspiration and a full exhalation breath is held for a few seconds. During normal breathing the puncture site is thoroughly cleaned with alcohol swabs and infiltrated with 5 ml 2% lignocaine. The skin is anaesthetised with a fine needle, which is replaced by a 21 gauge needle to infiltrate down to the liver capsule with the breath held in expiration.

There are two types of needle in general use and both provide adequate biopsy samples. The Menghini suction biopsy needle has been longer established and requires a shorter period of penetration of the liver. The Tru-Cut sheathed biopsy needle is slightly more cumbersome to use. An automatic needle (Biopty) does not confer any definite advantage.

Menghini needle

The Menghini needle is supplied in a variety of calibres and lengths. For routine use the 1.9×70 mm size is recommended. The slight theoretical advantage of smaller diameter needles is offset by the larger number of liver punctures required to obtain satisfactory tissue samples. The tip of the needle has a bevelled cutting edge. The needle is supplied with a blunt nail which fits inside the proximal shaft to prevent the sample being violently aspirated into the syringe, and with an external guard for the shaft to prevent too deep penetration of the liver; neither of these is essential. A trocar is also supplied and is non-contributory.

The needle is attached to a 20-ml syringe containing 5 ml physiological saline. A skin incision is made with a small-blade scalpel and the needle is advanced through the chest wall to the pleura and diaphragm. Saline (2 ml) is injected to clear the needle. The patient then performs the breath-holding manoeuvre. Aspiration is applied to the syringe and the needle is rapidly introduced about 4 cm into the liver and then immediately withdrawn. Thereupon the patient is permitted to breathe normally. The needle is removed from the syringe, the nail removed and the core of liver tissue is gently extruded either onto filter paper first or directly into formal saline, using the probe supplied. The contents of the syringe can be flushed through the needle into cytology fixative. If a satisfactory core (over 5 mm) is not obtained, then it is permitted to perform two more punctures at the same procedure.

Various modifications of the Menghini system are available. Disposable needles are usual. The Jamshidi needle is supplied with a locking syringe which does not require the operator to maintain traction on the plunger. The Surecut needle is also supplied with a locking syringe, to the plunger of which is attached a retractable trocar which obviates the need for saline injection.

Tru-Cut sheathed needle

This needle requires more skill in operation, but has become popular partly because of its wide application to other biopsy procedures such as sampling prostate and breast tissue.

The needle consists of an outer 2 mm cutting sheath through which is advanced a trocar with a 20-mm sampling groove positioned 10 mm from the tip. There is a choice of length of needle, of which the most convenient is 114 mm long.

After preparation, anaesthesia and skin incision with a scalpel, the needle is advanced to the liver capsule with the trocar retracted. The patient then holds the breath in expiration while the needle is advanced 4 cm into the liver with the trocar fully sheathed. The sheath is then retracted to permit a sample of liver to bulge into the trocar sampling groove. The cutting sheath is then fully advanced holding the trocar steady, and the whole needle is removed.

Operators are recommended to practise the sequence of manoeuvres several times before puncturing patients and to consult the manufacturer's instruction leaflet supplied with each needle.

This procedure is an amendment of a previous one, designed to improve safety. Needles must never been reused.

Alternative techniques

Bleeding tendency

If the prothrombin time is prolonged, a course of vitamin K 10 mg i.v. or i.m. daily for 3 days may cause it to return to normal. If the prothrombin time remains prolonged and the liver biopsy is mandatory, an infusion of 2 units of fresh frozen plasma before and during percutaneous biopsy ensures the safety of the procedure. Similarly, if low platelet counts persist, then the transfusion of six packs of platelets can be used to cover the procedure. In haemophilia the use of factor VIII transfusion has been described. It is possible to occlude the needle tract by injection of gelatin sponge.

Transvenous liver biopsy

This is an ingenious device, using transjugular hepatic vein catheterisation for biopsy of patients with bleeding diathesis. The principle is that any haemorrhage is contained in the patient's own circulation. The procedure should be reserved for centres with experience of the catheterisation technique. There is an appreciable failure rate and biopsy samples tend to be very small.

Laparoscopic liver biopsy

This is an alternative for the patient with a bleeding tendency, since direct haemostasis can be achieved. It allows targeted biopsy in non-homogenous liver disease and can be specially helpful in macronodular cirrhosis, lymphoma and metastatic disease. Naked-eye diagnosis should be confirmed by histology, though with experience reliable macroscopic diagnosis of cirrhosis is possible.

Laparotomy

Liver biopsy at laparotomy is best done with biopsy needles to avoid spurious conclusions from the histology of the unrepresentative peripheral samples obtained with scissors or scalpel. Ideally the biopsy should be taken at the first procedure after opening the peritoneum. A laparotomy should never be performed for the *sole* purpose of obtaining a liver biopsy.

Aftercare

Gentle local pressure may be needed to stop oozing of blood. The biopsy wound is covered with an adhesive dressing. The patient is asked to lie as much as possible in the right lateral position for 3 h. Pulse and blood pressure are recorded every 15 min for an hour, then hourly. The patient is warned to expect mild discomfort. If there is a severe pain at the biopsy site, in the epigastrium or right shoulder tip, then an injection of pethidine 25–100 mg i.m. is given.

The procedure is mainly performed as a day case for out-patients. This is quite safe as long as patients can be observed for some hours after the procedure. Facilities must be available in order to admit those who develop important complications.

Complications

Serious morbidity occurs in about 5% of patients. The most important determining factor is the number of liver punctures. *Pain* is the commonest complication and is usually transient. The major hazards are haemorrhage and bile leakage. Pneumothorax may also occur.

Bleeding into the pleura or peritoneum may require transfusion and open suturing. It is diagnosed by a rising pulse and falling blood pressure, without much pain. Bleeding is said to be more common from hepatoma. An intrahepatic haematoma is common and usually of no significance, although it may interfere with subsequent liver imaging techniques.

Bile leakage may occur from an intrahepatic gallbladder. It sometimes occurs from a large duct but this is uncommon if liver biopsy is avoided in extrahepatic cholestasis. Bile leakage usually causes pain and tachycardia; hypotension may also occur. Any serious bile leak requires early laparotomy, suturing and peritoneal toilet.

The mortality rate of liver biopsy is contentious, but is probably around 1 : 750 overall. The mortality rate depends on the type of patient undergoing biopsy and can be expected to be higher in patients with metastatic carcinoma. In practice, deaths do not seem to be a problem in people fit enough to be investigated as out-patients.

Indications

(1) Evaluation and monitoring of alcoholic liver disease.
(2) Diagnosis of cirrhosis, chronic autoimmune hepatitis, drug jaundice, haemochromatosis, hepatolenticular degeneration, amyloid and sarcoid.
(3) Diagnosis of hepatocellular carcinoma.
(4) Diagnosis of metastatic carcinoma and lymphoma.
(5) Diagnosis of hepatomegaly and splenomegaly.
(6) Establishment of the cause of intrahepatic cholestasis.
(7) Monitoring the progress of treatment in chronic hepatitis and iron and copper storage diseases.
(8) Confirmation of Dubin–Johnson syndrome (constitutional conjugated hyperbilirubinaemia).
(9) Estimation of liver enzyme activity, e.g. glucuronyl transferase.
(10) Occasionally in the diagnosis of tuberculosis and pyrexia of unknown origin.

Contraindications to percutaneous biopsy

Absolute contraindications are an uncooperative patient, gross ascites, and suspected hydatid disease, haemangioma or peliosis hepatica.

Relative contraindications are proved extrahepatic cholestasis and a persistent bleeding tendency.

INTERPRETATION

Macroscopic appearance

It is often helpful to inspect the core of tissue which has been obtained. *Normal liver* is light brown or purple in colour. In *fatty liver* the biopsy is pale yellow. In *metastatic carcinoma* there may be white areas. In *Dubin–Johnson syndrome* the biopsy is black, while in the conjugated hyperbilirubinaemia of the *Rotor syndrome* it is normal in colour.

In *cholestasis* dark bile plus a heavy greenish-yellow pigmentation may be evident. In *cirrhosis* the liver appears non-homogenous and granular, with a gritty feel as the biopsy needle is inserted.

After rapid inspection the liver tissue should be immersed in formol saline for light microscopy. Other procedures necessitate the tissue samples being processed separately. For electron microscopy 4% iced glutaraldehyde is satisfactory. For cytology 95% alcohol or other special fixative is used. For liver enzyme assay fresh tissue should be transported on ice; it should be frozen rapidly if there is to be a delay in the analysis.

Histology

The value of the procedure depends on the adequacy of the size of the sample and the ability and experience of the pathologist. It is possible to diagnose acute viral hepatitis on a 5 mm core, but at least 15 mm is preferable for a reliable diagnosis of cirrhosis and chronic autoimmune hepatitis. Percutaneous and operative needle biopsies yield comparable results. Needle biopsies taken immediately after death are satisfactory, but autopsy histology is often difficult to interpret because of the frequency of centrilobular ischaemic necrosis. Surgical 'knife and fork' specimens yield large quantities of tissue, but a polymorphonuclear infiltrate and subcapsular fibrosis are very common even in apparently healthy livers.

Normal

The liver is arranged in regular units called acini. These are arranged around portal tracts, with a sinusoidal structure of mainly single cell plates between them and the central veins. In the portal tract are a portal venule, an arteriole, bile ducts, lymphatics and connective tissue. The wall of liver cells adjacent to the portal tract is known as the limiting plate. Between the parenchymal cells and the endothelial cells is the space of Disse containing tissue fluid and collagen and reticulin fibres. In the sinusoidal wall are the periodic acid–Schiff-positive Kupffer reticuloendothelial cells, and also fat-storing stellate cells (lipocytes or Ito cells).

Some of the liver cells have double nuclei and some are polypoid, but mitotic figures are rare. Some nuclei contain glycogen. A few fat vacuoles occur in the cytoplasm, and there is little stainable iron. Near bile canaliculi brown granules of lipofuscin 'wear and tear' pigment are seen. With ageing, polyploidy becomes commoner, lipofuscin increases and portal tract connective tissue becomes denser.

Acute viral hepatitis

There is extensive liver cell necrosis, worse around the centrilobular areas. It may be focal or confluent. Degenerate cells swell and become granular in appearance. There are rounded refractile eosinophilic bodies which reflect shrunken hepatocytes (Councilman bodies). A monocytic infiltration is observed especially around the portal tract. Marked centrilobular cholestasis may be evident. Orcein staining demonstrates the presence of the virus, which can also be shown by immunofluorescence. Liver biopsy is fairly reliable in diagnosis of viral hepatitis but does not distinguish it from drug hepatitis, so that an adequate history is important. It may be misleading if a biopsy is taken very early in the course of viral hepatitis.

Drug reactions

The histology in drug injury is variable and depends upon the nature of the drug. With some anabolic steroids there is centrilobular bile stasis. In chlorpromazine-type injury of the liver there is centrilobular bile stasis with variable portal inflammation, atypical proliferation of the bile ductules and many eosinophils. In injury from monoamine oxidase inhibitors and halothane the histological picture is identical to that of viral hepatitis. An associated peripheral blood eosinophilia may give a clue to an idiosyncratic allergic drug reaction.

Cirrhosis

It is possible to obtain an apparently normal biopsy in cirrhosis which is macronodular, but as a general rule liver biopsy is a reliable method of proving the diagnosis.

The essential features are liver cell necrosis and nodular regeneration, with disorganisation of the normal hepatic architecture. The activity of the cirrhotic process, regardless of the aetiology, is assessed by the presence of piecemeal necrosis, which produces an irregular border to the nodules, cellular infiltration and bile duct proliferation. In inactive cirrhosis the nodules are smooth and well demarcated by relatively acellular fibrous bands.

Alcoholic liver disease

Abnormal liver histology is almost always associated with elevated gamma-GT (and ALT) levels in the serum, but the histological lesion cannot be predicted from the clinical features. Some biopsy samples show normal architecture, although cytology of aspirated fluid usually shows necrotic liver cells of variable nuclear size and excess lymphocytes. The most common finding is increased *fat* in the parenchymal cells, which may be severe. *Fat granulomas* may occur. In *alcoholic hepatitis* there is extensive focal necrosis of liver cells with excess fat vacuoles unlike viral hepatitis. *Mallory's hyaline bodies,* which stain deep reddish-purple with haematoxylin and eosin, are a helpful characteristic finding in both alcoholic hepatitis and cirrhosis, but they can occur in other conditions. Patients with alcoholic hepatitis may recover completely, die or develop cirrhosis. The presence of perivenular sclerosis in alcoholic hepatitis may predict the development of cirrhosis. By contrast, megamitochondria carry a good prognosis. *Alcoholic cirrhosis* is not always distinguishable from other forms of cirrhosis, but the presence of Mallory's hyaline is an important clue. Some patients with alcoholic liver disease develop *chronic active hepatitis* and *hepatoma.*

Extrahepatic biliary obstruction

This histological appearance depends upon the stage of the disease. In the early stages histology is reasonably specific with proliferation of the septal or interlobular bile ducts, local portal zone lymphocyte accumulations and peripheral cholestasis. At a later stage there is ductular destruction and encircling of the portal tracts by dense fibrous tissue. Eventually a form of cirrhosis ensues which is indistinguishable from cirrhosis of other types. Histology is graded I–IV, which predicts prognosis to some extent.

Chronic autoimmune hepatitis

Piecemeal necrosis of liver cells at the junction of connective tissue and parenchyma occurs, with extensive infiltrate of mononuclear cells (many of them plasma cells). Connective tissue increases and there is deposition of collagen to form new septa. The changes may be patchy throughout the liver.

Chronic persistent hepatitis

The main feature of inflammatory infiltration which is largely mononuclear and confined to the portal tract. Piecemeal necrosis and collagen deposition are absent.

Malignant disease

In 75% of *metastatic disease* needle biopsies can demonstrate the tumour, but more than one biopsy may be necessary. In *hepatocellular carcinoma* a similarly high diagnostic rate may be achieved. If the lesion is diffuse, blind biopsy is adequate, but if there is a discrete tumour a targeted biopsy on the basis of a liver scan (ultrasonic or CT) yields better results.

Sometimes cytology analysis of the washings from the Menghini needle shows malignant cells when the biopsy histology does not.

13

Liver Ultrasound, Isotope Tests and Radiology

The anatomy of the liver and spleen and the physiology of the portal circulation can be investigated in numerous ways. Some of the techniques are too specialised for general use, but many have found a place in routine diagnosis.

ULTRASONOGRAPHY (Figure 30)

Ultrasound scanning (US) of the liver is a simple and reliable test for focal disease and for extra-hepatic obstruction. Ideally a complete upper abdominal scan should be performed when liver scanning is requested, since valuable information about the gallbladder, bile ducts and pancreas may also be gained.

Interpretation

Liver metastases

Discrete echogenic areas and focal hypoechoic areas are the most common findings, but the patterns are extremely variable. Solid metastases over 2 cm in diameter and cystic ones larger than 1 cm are reliably detected. The lateral right lobe of the liver is easiest to scan. Tumours up to 3–4 cm may be missed occasionally in other areas. The accuracy of ultrasonography in metastatic disease is about 80–90% and it is probably as good as or better than isotope scanning. Simple measurement of serum alkaline phosphatase has been reported to give similar results in known carcinomas, and this biochemical test may yet be the best method of screening for hepatic malignancy.

Hepatocellular carcinoma

This may be difficult to delineate. The ultrasonic consistency of the tumour may be similar to surrounding parenchyma, and the tumour may be diffuse with multiple small abnormal areas. A diagnostic success rate of around 60% is feasible with experience.

Cysts and abscesses

Ultrasonography is a very effective method of demonstrating hepatic cysts, and liver, subphrenic and other abdominal abscesses. Up to 100% accuracy

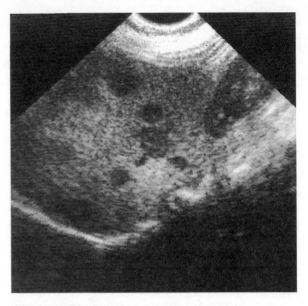

Figure 30 Ultrasonogram. Liver metastases

in defining liver cysts and abscesses is possible, and guided aspiration is readily performed if desired.

Jaundice

Ultrasonography is an extremely useful diagnostic tool in a patient with features suggestive of cholestatic jaundice.

The intrahepatic ducts are visualised only when dilated to a calibre of 4 mm or more. If extrahepatic ducts are of normal calibre they are seen in 60–80% of patients. Dilated extrahepatic ducts are regularly seen (<6–8 mm is the normal range; <10 mm if there has been a previous cholecystectomy). In extrahepatic obstruction, dilation of the extrahepatic ducts precedes dilation of the intrahepatic ducts. In intrahepatic cholestasis the bile ducts are usually normal, but there may be some dilation of intrahepatic (but not of extrahepatic) ducts.

There are some drawbacks to ultrasonography. Common duct stones, sclerosing cholangitis and ampullary strictures may escape detection; the distal common bile duct is obscured by bowel gas in some patients; enlargement of the pancreatic head may be due to either carcinoma or chronic pancreatitis; and gallstones may be incidental findings unrelated to the cause of jaundice. *Endosonography* is especially useful for detecting bile duct stones and pancreatic carcinomas.

Diffuse disease

High-amplitude echoes are found in *micronodular cirrhosis*, but also occur in fatty liver, hepatitis and congestive cardiac failure. This has been termed the 'bright liver'. The appearance is non-specific and insensitive, being often absent in macronodular cirrhosis, and ultrasonography is not recommend as a sole diagnostic procedure if these diseases are suspected. Portal hypertension and thrombosis of the portal and hepatic veins can also be detected.

Venography

Variceal and portal venous blood flow can be assessed by ultrasound, especially if Doppler techniques are used.

Main indications

(1) Diagnosis of cholestatic jaundice
(2) Diagnosis of cysts and abscesses
(3) Diagnosis of liver metastases
(4) Assessment of portal blood flow and venous thrombosis

ISOTOPE SCANNING

In many departments isotopic liver scanning has been largely replaced by the more informative ultrasonic scanning as a rapid and simple technique for screening the liver. It remains useful in the assessment of cirrhosis with portal hypertension, diagnosis of large liver tumours and definition of liver and spleen size. The isotope most commonly used is the gamma-emitting technetium-99m, which can either be administered as a colloidal sulphide or as a labelled macroaggregate of albumin. The isotope is taken up by the Kupffer cells and has a half-life of 6 h. Indium-113m colloid is an equivalent alternative.

Method

No special preparation of the patient is necessary and the patient need not be fasting. The patient is scanned in the supine position, and both anteroposterior and lateral scans are obtained. Scanning is commenced about 15 min after the intravenous injection of the isotope, when stabilisation of the count rate indicates that maximal radioactivity has been reached over the liver. The scanning procedure takes about 20 min depending upon the size of the liver. Upon completion of the procedure the surface markings of the costal margins, xiphisternum and the liver, if enlarged, are marked on the scan to aid its interpretation.

Interpretation

Normal liver. There is good, even uptake of the isotope with the maximum activity being registered over the right lobe. The spleen is clearly outlined with ^{99m}Tc. The distribution of isotope between liver and spleen gives some assessment of liver function.

Cirrhosis. A patchy appearance may be seen and when this is marked the liver may appear to have a number of filling defects. This has given rise to diagnostic difficulties with diffuse hepatic secondaries or even hypertension. Liver size may be either greatly reduced or increased.

Portal hypertension with collateral circulation. A characteristic pattern is seen: the small liver has a poor uptake, the large spleen avidly concentrates the ^{99m}Tc and there is clear outlining of the vertebral bodies.

Metastases. Areas of low activity are seen. Metastases of more than 3 cm are usually seen, but the technique has a lower overall sensitivity of about 60%. Isotope scans do not differentiate between metastases, abscesses and cysts.

Hepatocellular carcinoma. This shows on the ^{99m}Tc scan as a filling defect, which may be rounded or extend as processes from the porta hepatis. A second scan with selenium-75 methionine or gallium-67 citrate shows the hepatocellular carcinoma as a 'hot' area, and subtraction of the scans gives a positive result in 90% or more cases. *Hepatic abscesses* and *metastases* may show the same pattern, but the technique is not so reliable in these diseases and the ^{99m}Tc scan may be negative.

Indications

(1)   To define liver and spleen position and size and function
(2)   Diagnosis of cirrhosis with portal hypertension, especially where biopsy is not possible
(3)   Diagnosis of hepatocellular carcinoma

RADIOLOGY

Plain abdominal radiograph

A film of the abdomen is useful in determining the liver and spleen size. An enlarged liver frequently causes diaphragmatic elevation although an enlarged spleen does not. Calcification in the liver substance is seen in benign tumours, particularly haemangiomas, and in malignant tumours, abscesses and hydatid cysts. Less than 50% of hepatic hydatid cysts show calcification which may appear as a thin rim over part or all of the cyst surface, or the cyst may be extensively calcified in a reticular pattern. Air may be seen in the biliary tract and the identification of calcified gallstones is of help in the icteric patient.

Barium studies

A barium swallow is of help in the identification of oesophageal varices, which are best demonstrated when the lower oesophagus is coated with a thin layer of barium. The oesophagus is slightly dilated and there are numerous filling defects which distort the vertical mucosal folds. Oesophageal candida can give similar appearances.

The presence of varices indicates the opening of portasystemic anastomotic channels and is a sign of portal hypertension. Varices are present when there is either intra- or extra-hepatic obstruction to the portal circulation and do not necessarily indicate hepatic cirrhosis. They may be seen in the acute fatty liver, infectious and alcoholic hepatitis, and presinusoidal causes of portal hypertension such as schistosomiasis.

Computed tomography

This procedure provides good images of the liver and can demonstrate space-occupying lesions such as tumours, cysts and abscesses, as well as fatty liver. It is superior to isotope scanning and at least equivalent to ultrasonic scanning. Results can be improved by use of X-ray contrast. Spiral CT is superior because it avoids misregistration problems from multiple breath holds.

Magnetic resonance imaging (MRI) (Figure 31)

Though not universally available, MRI is superior to ultrasonography and isotope scanning in liver disease because of its greater sensitivity. It is probably also superior to computed tomography, and is likely to become more so with the development of technical advances and the use of contrast media, such as gadolinium-DTPA and superparamagnetic ferrite-iron oxide particles.

Arteriography

Selective coeliac arteriography is of value in the investigation of patients with liver disease. The technique can be used to distinguish between benign lesions (such as hydatid cysts) and malignant tumours, which produce a characteristic distortion of the hepatic arterioles. The vasculature is also distorted in the cirrhotic liver. It can be used to outline the portal vein in patients who have undergone splenectomy or when splenic venography is contraindicated. The tip of the catheter is placed in the orifice of the superior mesenteric artery and contrast agent injected while imaging rapidly. The technique presents few problems for the radiological department versed in angiographic techniques.

Selective mesenteric arteriography has been used to define the collateral circulation in portal hypertension and to enable the direct infusion of pitressin to control haemorrhage. It is also used pre-operatively to assist planning of surgery.

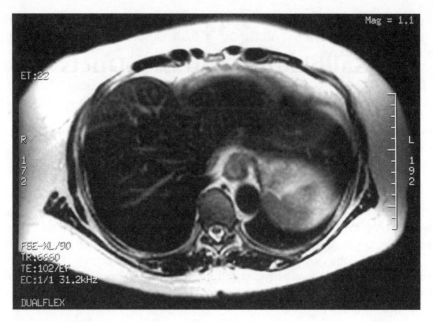

Figure 31 Magnetic resonance imaging (MRI). Carcinoma of the oesophagus. Normal liver

DIAGNOSIS OF CHOLESTASIS

There are many different causes of cholestasis, manifested by jaundice, itching, dark urine, conjugated hyperbilirubinaemia, and raised serum alkaline phosphatase and gamma-GT. If the cause is extrahepatic, persistent and surgically remediable, it is important to proceed to surgery promptly to avoid secondary hepatocellular failure. By contrast, if the cause is intrahepatic then operation is contraindicated, both because of the possibility of causing liver and renal failure and the absence of useful relieving surgical procedures.

The most common causes of extrahepatic obstruction are common bile duct gallstones and carcinoma of the head of the pancreas. The most common causes of intrahepatic cholestasis are alcoholic liver disease, drug toxicity, viral liver disease, and metastases. Rapid and safe diagnosis is essential if the correct management is to be employed. Sclerosing cholangitis and co-existing intrahepatic and extrahepatic causes for cholestasis may give rise to diagnostic problems.

At present the major techniques for the diagnosis of cholestasis are ultrasonic scanning, endoscopic retrograde cholangiopancreatography, percutaneous transhepatic cholangiography, computed tomography, MRI scanning and laparoscopy. The latter is the least useful.

14

Gallbladder and Bile Ducts

Investigation of the biliary tree depends mainly on the demonstration of anatomical changes by radiology or ultrasonic scanning techniques. Serum biochemistry may lend support to diagnosis, but is usually non-specific.

ULTRASONOGRAPHY (Figure 32)

Ultrasonic scanning is very rapid and simple to perform, and yields a 96% accuracy for gallbladder gallstones.

Gallstones over 3 mm in size can be detected as mobile structures within the gallbladder, whose wall is often thickened. Those stones over 5 mm in diameter produce prominent acoustic shadows which assist interpretation. The presence of calcium in stones increases the ultrasonic definition.

The thickness of the gallbladder wall may be a clue to disease. It is 2 mm or less in 97% of asymptomatic subjects without gallstones and greater than 3 mm in 45% with gallstone disease. Large carcinomas of the gallbladder are readily seen, as are mucoceles.

Failure to obtain an image of the gallbladder is uncommon, but may also be a sign of disease.

Ultrasonography is useful for measuring bile duct calibre but is not as accurate as endoscopic retrograde cholangiopancreatography (ERCP) for detecting duct stones. It readily defines choledochal cysts in children. Ultrasonography can be employed at laparotomy using a transducer held adjacent to bile ducts and pancreas. This could replace the operative cholangiogram.

Ultrasonic gallbladder scanning is very useful for evaluation of the non-functioning gallbladder or after a failed cholecystogram. High-definition real-time scanning largely replaces the oral cholecystogram as a first-line test but the techniques are complementary.

Endosonography

This technique is not freely available at present, but offers the best chance of detecting common bile duct stones without introducing iodine contrast directly into the biliary system. Biliary tumours and strictures can also be identified. It may eventually replace ERCP in diagnosis, and could be used as a screen preliminary to therapeutic ERCP.

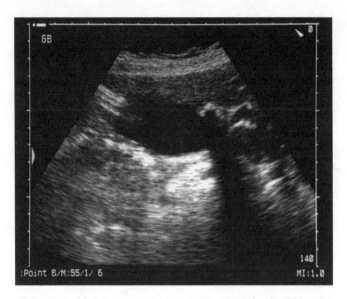

Figure 32 Ultrasonogram. Large stone in neck of gallbladder

PLAIN RADIOLOGY

Between 10 and 20% of gallstones are sufficiently calcified to be visible on the upper right side of the abdomen. Sometimes the calcification is homogenous, but often it shows an internal laminar pattern which is helpful in diagnosis. Gallstones may either have rounded contours, or straight edges if they have been pressed against other stones. Multiple small irregular calcified stones are frequently composed of calcium bilirubinate. Pure cholesterol stones are radiolucent.

Occasionally large gallstones show internal fractures with hyperlucent lines radiating from the centre. This is called the tri-fin or Mercedes-Benz sign and can be detected even in the absence of calcification. The position of gallstones usually requires confirmation by supplementary procedures.

Calcium deposits are occasionally seen in the gallbladder wall: the 'porcelain gallbladder'. Even less often, bile contains a large amount of calcium salts in suspension: 'limy' or 'milk of calcium' bile, which outlines the biliary tree.

Gas in the biliary tree occurs in infections with gas-forming organisms and when it affects the gallbladder is called *emphysematous cholecystitis*. It also occurs when there is a fistula between the intestine and gallbladder or bile ducts and after some operations to the biliary tree. Gas can also occur when there is an incompetent sphincter of Oddi, which may result from sphincterotomy.

ORAL CHOLECYSTOGRAPHY (Figure 33)

Oral cholecystography is less useful in acute cholecystitis when non-functioning gallbladders and cystic duct obstruction occur.

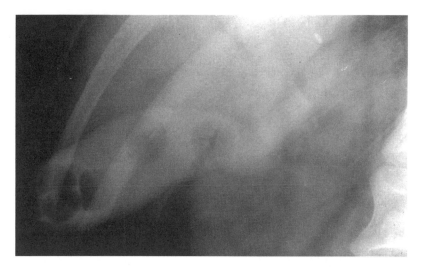

Figure 33 Oral cholecystogram. Gallbladder stones with Mercedes-Benz sign (trifin fracture)

Method

A plain radiography of the abdomen is taken prior to ingesting the contrast medium. An opaque medium is administered orally, and this is absorbed from the intestinal tract, excreted by the liver, concentrated in the gallbladder and discharged via the bile ducts into the intestine. A variety of tri-iodo organic iodine compounds may be used for this purpose and a popular agent is sodium iopadate. This is taken as tablets with a normal evening meal on the evening before the examination. Thereafter, the patient is asked to fast until the radiographic examination the following day.

An alternative technique is to use the same dose spread out over 1–2 days prior to the examination. This may yield a higher proportion of positive results at the first examination.

Some departments routinely use a laxative with the preparation. As this may interfere with the absorption of the contrast medium, and as intestinal gas causes much more difficulty with interpretation than faeces, it cannot be recommended.

Radiographic films of the full gallbladder are obtained between 12 and 16 h after the ingestion of the opaque medium, including films in both erect and horizontal postures. In cases of poor opacification tomography is helpful.

Gallbladder contraction is then stimulated by either a physiological stimulus such as eating two eggs, a cheese roll or a bar of chocolate, or by slow intravenous injection of cholecystokinin (CCK 33 units.) Larger doses of CCK and proprietary emulsions cannot be recommended as they are very prone to causing abdominal distress and vomiting. Caerulin is an alternative pharmaceutical preparation but has no definite practical advantages. Further radiographic films are taken after gallbladder contraction, which occurs 30–60 min after an oral stimuli and 10–20 min after intravenous CCK.

Contraction films may show calculi which were not visible in the filled gallbladder, and it is at this stage that it may be possible to visualise the cystic duct. The common bile duct is only occasionally delineated clearly by oral cholecystography. Failure of gallbladder function on cholecystography is not certain evidence for disease, and it is advisable to repeat the examination at least once. This may conveniently be done after an initial series of films following a 3-g dose of iopanic acid by giving a further dose of 3 g iopanic acid on the day of the unsatisfactory examination and repeating the films the next day. Alternatively, some other test such as ultrasonography or infusion cholangiography should be undertaken.

Interpretation

There are two definite oral cholecystogram appearances which demonstrate unequivocal evidence of organic gallbladder disease. One is when there are gallbladder stones, and the other is the presence of contrast in the bile ducts but no gallbladder filling.

In 5% of examinations there is evidence of some abnormality of the gallbladder wall such as cholesterolosis, adenomyomatosis, papillomas, prominent spiral valves and a 'Phrygian cap'. These occur independently of gallstones and cholecystitis, and are not proof of symptomatic biliary disease.

Cholesterolosis of the gallbladder is suspected when there is an uneven mucosal contour with single or multiple filling detects. *Adenomyomatosis* of the gallbladder may show as a solitary filling defect; as a segmental stricture, which must be distinguished from a 'Phrygian cap' (in which the septum is thinner and the distal segment contracts proportionately with the proximal segment); and as a diffuse condition which can be recognised by the contrast-filled Rokitansky–Aschoff sinuses. In *cancer of the gallbladder* there is usually no function of the gallbladder, which generally contains gallstones.

A meticulous radiological technique is required for oral cholecystography and, given this, it is one of the most accurate of radiological investigations. The method can detect abnormality with a 95–99% accuracy. It gives positive evidence of 70% and presumptive evidence of 98–99% of gallstones, and probably detects 95% of significant cholecystitis.

Failure to outline the gallbladder also occurs if there is impaired absorption of the contrast medium. This may result from vomiting, delayed gastric emptying and diarrhoea. In such circumstances no conclusions can be drawn regarding gallbladder function. Oral cholecystography is not undertaken when there is liver cell dysfunction, because no satisfactory excretion of the dye is obtained when the serum conjugated bilirubin concentration is greater than 50 μmol/l. Difficulty may also occur in anicteric patients with cholestasis. In the absence of the parenchymal liver disease or hypermotility of the gut the failure to visualise the gallbladder after two attempts at cholecystography (the second being with a double dose of the contrast agent) may be accepted as evidence that the organ is diseased. The technique should be avoided in renal failure, where it is often ineffective and also hazardous.

OPERATIVE CHOLANGIOGRAPHY

At the time of cholecystectomy the cystic duct is cannulated and iodine contrast such as diatrizoate is injected. Good images of the common duct and both hepatic ducts are obtained. This procedure eliminates the risk of unsuspected retained stones, known to occur in up to 4% of patients who are followed after cholecystectomy. It also detects the rare bile duct carcinomas. At present the consensus view is that operative cholangiography should be considered in all patients undergoing cholecystectomy for gallstones unless there has been careful pre-operation screening with ERCP. Digital subtraction techniques improve image quality.

Both flexible and rigid choledochoscopes (cholangioscopes) are available for the same purpose; these usually require the common duct to be opened for their insertion and do not offer entirely satisfactory views of the distal common bile duct. Direct per-operative ultrasonography is another option.

Where duct stones have been removed it is usual to leave a T-tube in place and to confirm clearing of calculi by repeating the cholangiogram through the tube immediately before it is removed (Figure 34).

PERCUTANEOUS TRANSHEPATIC CHOLANGIOGRAPHY (PTC)

Where ERCP is not possible or fails, this remains a definitive procedure for precise localisation of the cause of extrahepatic obstruction before an abdominal operation is undertaken. However, ultrasonography and computed tomography can often provide similar information.

Method

The patient is prepared as for a liver biopsy. It is important that a surgeon is informed when the procedure is to take place so that a laparotomy, if needed, can be performed without undue delay. Bile leakage and septicaemia may occur, even with the fine Chiba needle, and antibiotic cover starting immediately before the procedure is prudent. Gentamicin 80 mg and ampicillin 1 g is commonly used. Studies of blood haemostasis should be normal, as for liver biopsy.

The patient is placed supine on the radiology table and the procedure is carried out under fluoroscopy. The needle is 15 cm long, 0.7 cm external diameter and fitted with a stylet. It is flexible so that the patient can breathe normally when it is in position.

The skin is punctured in the 7th–8th right intercostal space in the mid-axillary line. The needle is advanced parallel to the table and is aimed two

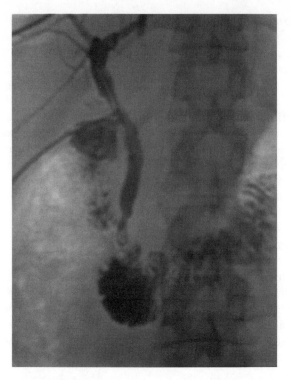

Figure 34 T-tube cholangiogram. Bile duct stone

vertebral bodies below the junction of the diaphragm with the spine. After advancing fully the stylet is withdrawn. Because it may not be possible to aspirate bile even when the needle tip is positioned correctly, it is preferable to connect a syringe containing 50 ml of a low osmolar iodinated contrast via flexible tubing and inject a little contrast continuously as the needle is slowly withdrawn. Flow is centripetal in bile ducts, as distinct from the centrifugal flow of dye injected into portal veins, and the midline drainage in the hepatic veins. While a bile duct is entered, contrast is injected and films are taken. If the needle is completely withdrawn without a bile duct being identified, five more attempts are permitted, using different puncture sites separated by 3–5 cm. Post-procedure care is similar to that for a liver biopsy. If there is evidence of a bile leak immediate surgery may be required.

Interpretation

The procedure identifies dilated ducts in almost all of cases, and has the added advantage of usually identifying the precise cause of obstruction. It also succeeds in demonstrating ducts in 65% of 'non-surgical' disorders. The technique is so accurate that if dilated ducts cannot be demonstrated, further evidence of extrahepatic obstruction in the jaundiced patient is required before undertaking a laparotomy. The overall mortality is 0.5% and morbidity is 5%. Fever occurs in 3.5% of cases, hypotension in 2%, bile leakage in 2.5% and bleeding in 1%.

In specialist centres PTC has an additional role, being used either for external biliary drainage or to insert a prosthesis in patients with malignant obstruction of the biliary tree, or to remove gallstones.

Transjugular cholangiography is feasible for the patient who has a bleeding tendency. Where PTC fails, *laparoscopy* or *minilaparotomy* enables direct cholangiography before proceeding to full laparotomy.

Indications

(1)   Diagnosis of cholestasis
(2)   Diagnosis of biliary strictures
(3)   Diagnosis of hepatic duct carcinoma
(4)   Positioning of guide-wires and biliary stents and drains

COMPUTED TOMOGRAPHY

This gives good results in gallstone disease, gallbladder cancer and obstructive jaundice, but other cheaper techniques do so too and should normally be the first choice.

A special use is in the evaluation of stones for non-surgical therapy. Radiolucent stones may have significant calcification precluding a successful dissolution therapy, and this is indicated by CT density greater than 90 Hounsfield units. Since this type of treatment can be very prolonged it is helpful to use CT as a screen to exclude some of the cases where failure can be predicted.

MAGNETIC RESONANCE IMAGING (Figure 35)

It seems likely that MRI will eventually reach the stage where it is possible to make exact chemical analyses of stones within the patient. In other circumstances it is equivalent to CT. MRI cholangiopancreatography (MRCP) is very promising but still under evaluation for bile duct and pancreatic disease.

ISOTOPE SCANNING

Biliary scintigraphy

Technetium-99m compounds have been developed which are rapidly excreted by the liver even in the presence of cholestatic obstructive jaundice. Two which have been well evaluated are ^{99m}Tc-labelled dimethyl-acetanilide

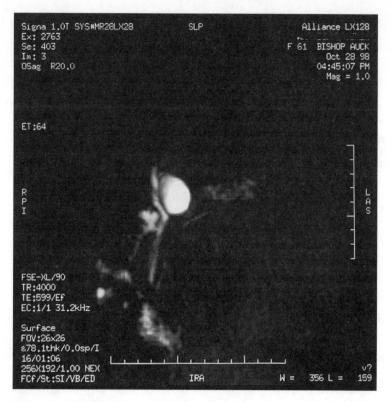

Figure 35 Normal magnetic resonance cholangiopancreatogram (MRCP). Gallbladder, CBD, common hepatic and left hepatic bile ducts, pancreatic duct and pancreas

iminodiacetic acid (^{99m}Tc-HIDA) and ^{99m}Tc-labelled pyridoxylidene glutamate (^{99m}Tc-PG). There are many others. The procedure is used for the diagnosis of acute cholecystitis and is helpful in the differential diagnosis of acute abdominal pain. Scans should be performed within 48 h of symptoms.

Method

The patient is fasted for 4 h and then 50 MBq ^{99m}Tc-Pg or 80 MBq of ^{99m}Tc-HIDA is normally injected intravenously; more is used if the patient is icteric. The patient is then scanned by gamma-camera with dynamic studies and serial photographs every 10 min for 1 h. If no gallbladder image is seen then the scan is repeated at 3–4 h. If desired the nature of a gallbladder image may be confirmed by scanning 1–20 min after intravenous CCK 33 units.

Interpretation

A positive scan (no gallbladder activity) is always seen in *acute cholecystitis*, and in about half the patients with other gallbladder diseases. A negative scan (gallbladder activity) excludes acute cholecystitis, but does not necessarily mean the gallbladder is normal.

In infancy failure of excretion after liver uptake indicates *biliary atresia*. This technique has a particular role in the diagnosis of persistent cholestatic jaundice in the early months of life. Some 60% of such patients have biliary atresia which may require surgery, but 25% have neonatal hepatitis of one form or another and this is a contraindication to operative intervention.

Gallbladder white blood cell scanning

An alternative technique is labelling and re-injection of leukocytes with ^{99m}Tc-HMPAO. Images are taken over the gallbladder about hourly for 4 h, and then at 24 h. In *acute cholecystitis* activity concentrates in the inflamed gallbladder wall in the first 4 h.

15

Ascites and the Peritoneum

The aetiology of ascites may be obvious from the history and physical examination. However, it is generally necessary to examine the fluid microscopically, chemically and bacteriologically. Even when the cause is clinically apparent, for example hepatic cirrhosis and portal hypertension, it may not be possible to exclude either super-imposed infection or hepatocellular cancer.

PARACENTESIS

Diagnostic paracentesis is a simple technique and can easily be undertaken in all patients presenting for the first time with ascites unless there is a specific contraindication.

Method

The patient should be asked to empty the bladder if not catheterised. The usual site for aspiration is in the right or left lower quadrant midway between the umbilicus and the anterior superior iliac spine. A 21-gauge needle may be used to inject the local anaesthetic and a similar size needle can then be inserted through the peritoneum for the paracentesis. Other suitable needles are those used for lumbar and cisternal puncture. When there is a very tense ascites it is often possible to insert a fine needle without using local anaesthetic. After a sufficient volume of fluid has been withdrawn for examination the needle is removed and a gauze dressing is applied to the wound.

Complications

These are rare. Occasionally an abdominal wall vein is penetrated. The procedure may be followed by a leak of fluid from the injection site when the ascites is very tense. A skin suture after aspiration may prevent this, but not infrequently the leak only stops when the ascites has been relieved.

Interpretation

Appearance

Ascites fluid which is a *transudate* is clear and straw-coloured. An *exudate* may also be clear but the fluid is often cloudy and opalescent because of a high cell content. Trauma, malignant disease or tuberculous disease of the peritoneum may cause the fluid to be bloodstained. The fluid has a high mucoid content when pseudomucinous tumours have invaded the peritoneum.

Microscopic examination

Ascitic fluid, 5 ml, is added to a tube containing anticoagulant, centrifuged for 10 min and a smear made of the deposit. A rough estimate is made of the number of cells and a differential count is undertaken. The presence of many polymorphonuclear leucocytes suggests non-tuberculous infection while a high lymphocyte count suggests tuberculosis or lymphoma. The unstained smear may be examined for microfilaria and trypanosomes, or it can be fixed and stained with either Leishman or Giemsa stain.

The spun deposit may be stained and examined for malignant cells by a trained cytopathologist. An accuracy of about 86% correct positive diagnosis is achieved. There is much difficulty in identifying cells when there has been ascites of long duration such as with cirrhosis of the liver. Exfoliated mesothelial cells are a particular cause of confusion and can be mistaken for malignant cells.

A counting chamber can be used for cell counts, but caution must be exercised in the interpretation of the result when there is contamination with red blood cells.

In *transudates*, for example alcoholic liver disease, the mean cell count is $280/mm^3$.

In *exudates* the count is usually over $500/mm^3$. Exudates associated with carcinoma have an average cell count of $690/mm^3$ (with mixed cellularity); tuberculous exudates characteristically many lymphocytes (92%).

Two conditions with very high counts, averaging $7000/mm^3$, are lymphomas where nearly 70% of cells are lymphocytes, and spontaneous peritonitis in which the cells are almost entirely polymorphs. If the count is less than $250/mm^3$ the ascites is sterile, and peritonitis can only be confidently diagnosed when counts exceed $1000/mm^3$.

Chemical analysis

A *protein content* of less than 25 g/l suggests that the fluid is a *transudate*. This is usually the case in heart failure, cirrhosis of the liver, nephrosis and other conditions associated with severe hypoproteinaemia.

A protein concentration greater than 25 g/l suggests the presence of an *exudate*. This is found in acute peritoneal infections, tuberculous peritonitis and metastatic malignant disease involving the peritoneum. Occasionally a high protein content is encountered in cirrhosis in the absence of infection or malignant disease. The ascitic fluid may contain a high protein content in patients with myxoedema and endomyocardial fibrosis.

The *amylase* concentration of the ascitic fluid may be increased in patients with acute pancreatitis and pancreatic pseudocyst. Occasionally a perforated peptic ulcer will be associated with amylase-rich ascitic fluid.

Bacteriological examination

At least 10–20 ml of the ascitic fluid is sent for culture. When tuberculosis is suspected a large volume of the fluid is sent to the laboratory in a bottle containing sodium citrate to prevent the fluid from clotting. TB may be sought by smear, culture or guinea-pig inoculation, but the diagnosis of tuberculous peritonitis is established by bacteriological methods in only 50% of patients.

Diagnostic paracentesis in the acute abdomen

The technique is a modification of that used when there is ascites. A 21-gauge needle is inserted under local anaesthesia into the peritoneal cavity at four sites: the right and left upper and lower quadrants midway between the umbilicus and the anterior superior iliac spines below and the ninth costal cartilage above. Gentle suction is applied using a 2 or 5 ml syringe while the needle is moved about within the peritoneal cavity. The appearance and volume of the aspirate is noted and the material sent for biochemical and bacteriological analysis.

Normally less than 0.5 ml clear fluid can be aspirated. A positive result is obtained when the volume exceeds 0.5 ml or when the fluid is obviously abnormal. This suggests intra-abdominal disease. A negative paracentesis has no diagnostic significance. The technique is of value in the diagnosis of *acute intraperitoneal haemorrhage* as in acute pancreatitis when pure blood is aspirated that fails to clot.

Paracentesis is especially helpful in the management of patients with non-penetrating abdominal injury. Alkaline bile-stained fluid, often containing food debris, is characteristic of a *perforated peptic ulcer*. The technique is not of value in the diagnosis of localised inflammatory disease.

The procedure is safe although the intestine may be accidentally penetrated when there are many adhesions or if there is a malignant peritonitis. This is usually readily appreciated from the appearance and microscope of the aspirate.

Chylous ascites

The aspiration of an opalescent, cloudy fluid suggests the possibility of a chylous ascites which follows a leak of lymph into the peritoneal cavity. Chylous fluid contains absorbed fat (>5 mmol/l) in the form of particulate chylomicrons which float on standing. This must be distinguished from pseudocylous ascitic fluid which is opalescent because it contains fat and granular material derived from degenerated cells (which tend to sediment).

Chronic chylous ascites is associated with malignancy in 80% of cases. A wide variety of cases may underlie subacute chylous ascites.

PERITONEAL BIOPSY

Peritoneal biopsy is a most helpful technique for investigating unexplained ascites. It is simple and safe and is of particular value in the diagnosis of tuberculous peritonitis.

Method

The biopsy is obtained from the right or left lower quadrant lateral to the rectus sheath. A small area of the abdominal wall is anaesthetised using 1% procaine hydrochloride and the needle is introduced into the peritoneal cavity. It is advisable to discontinue the procedure if ascitic fluid is not aspirated readily. A small incision is made in the skin and the biopsy needle is introduced. When there is a little fluid an assistant applies contralateral abdominal pressure to ensure the largest possible volume of fluid at the biopsy site. One or several portions of the peritoneum are taken from different quadrants of the same biopsy site, the Cope needle being suitable for obtaining more than one specimen. The needle is withdrawn and a tight dressing applied. The wound may be sutured if there is much ascites. The biopsy specimen is removed from the needle and placed in 10% formal saline.

Types of needle

A Tru-Cut needle can be used but is less satisfactory than the side-biting, hook-type needles of the type described by Cope and by Abrams.

Cope needle. This needle consists of a trocar, biopsy shaft and snare. After penetrating the peritoneum the trocar is removed, ascitic fluid is aspirated for examination and the snare is introduced. The instrument is withdrawn until the snare engages the peritoneum. A biopsy is obtained by a forward-rotating advance of the biopsy shaft. The snare with the excised tissue is withdrawn and may be re-inserted if further samples are required from a particular site.

Abrams needle. This needle comprises two concentric tubes. The outer tube has a short trocar point behind which is a deep notch which can be closed by the inner tube. The inner tube has a cutting edge. A spring clip holds a pin on the base of the inner tube in either the open or closed position. The back hexagonal grip is twisted anti-clockwise so that the notch is opened and a sample of the ascitic fluid is aspirated. When this is completed the needle is withdrawn until the notch is felt to engage the peritoneum. The outer tube is held steady and the back hexagonal grip is twisted sharply clockwise to pinch off a portion of peritoneum. The apparatus is withdrawn and the biopsy specimen is found either in the hollow point or inside the cutting cylinder.

Forceps biopsy. Where a trocar is placed for therapeutic paracentesis, endoscopy forceps can be introduced until resistance is reached, then opened and closed.

Complications

It is unusual for peritoneal biopsy to be associated with any complication if the biopsy is performed when there is ascites. Haemorrhage or a leak of ascitic fluid can be prevented by a pressure dressing or sutures.

LAPAROSCOPY (PERITONEOSCOPY)

This is a very useful technique for diagnosis of ascites because not only are the peritoneum and abdominal organs inspected, but biopsies can be obtained from the peritoneum and liver.

The procedure has been performed in humans since 1910. Despite this and its popularity in Europe and in the USA, it was not widely used for the investigation of gastrointestinal disease in Britain until the advent of laparoscopic surgery.

Laparoscopy permits the visualisation of the anterior surface of the liver, with the exception of the right lateral aspect, together with its leading edges and inferior surface. The anterior surface of the gallbladder and stomach can be seen, together with parts of the small bowel, colon and mesentery. The peritoneum over the diaphragm, anterior abdominal wall and falciform ligament are seen. The pancreas can be seen by lifting the left lobe of the liver. The pelvic organs (bladder, uterus, Fallopian tubes and ovaries) can be seen with the patient in the Trendelenburg position. With patience almost all of the small bowel can be reviewed.

Method

Instruments

There are many forward- and oblique-viewing instruments, some with an operating channel for biopsy needles and probes. The fibre-optic light system is usually employed, and most instruments are insulated to permit diathermy. Instruments currently in general use are rigid, but flexible ones are available. The equipment consists of a trocar, sheath, telescope and light source. Air is insufflated through a Veress needle with retractable cannula, and this can be either via an automatic insufflator or a sterile sphygmomanometer bulb. Pre-warming in an oven or on an electrical pad, and use of an anti-fogging liquid on the lens are convenient. Cleaning should be followed by ethylene oxide or activated glutaraldehyde sterilisation between cases.

Procedure

This is best performed on a table with full tilting facilities.

The patient is premedicated with an analgesic and tranquilliser such as pethidine 50–100 mg and midazolam 5 mg i.v. with the procedure. Doses should be reduced in liver disease. General anaesthetic is an alternative, but this negates one advantage of laparoscopy over laparotomy. The operator prepares by scrubbing, and wears gown and gloves as for major surgery. A puncture site is selected, avoiding epigastric vessels and visible collateral veins, abdominal scars and the falciform ligament. The standard site is 2–4 cm inferior to the umbilicus in the midline. If better vision of the liver is needed then the puncture should be to the left or the midline above the umbilicus.

The skin and subcutaneous tissue are anaesthetised as far as the parietal peritoneum if possible. A vertical incision is made to admit the trocar through the skin and fascia. The Veress needle is inserted through the wound and advanced carefully into the peritoneal cavity. When the tip is in place the needle is laid flat on the skin, and moderate distension of the abdomen with air or CO_2 is achieved (about 2–3 litres usually). The Veress needle is then removed and the peritoneoscope sheath (with trocar inserted) is passed into the peritoneum cavity. This requires force, and should be carried out with the table lowered and the arms of the operator extended fully to avoid sudden excessive penetration. When the peritoneal cavity has been entered the trocar is removed immediately. The sheath should be freely mobile when the telescope is passed. The room is darkened and the systematic inspection begins. It is important to remember that touching the falciform ligament and parietal peritoneum causes pain.

The liver, gallbladder, falciform ligament, parietal peritoneum and inferior surface of stomach and bowel should be inspected routinely. The spleen is seen only if enlarged. The pancreas may be seen with special manoeuvres. Pelvic organs can also be inspected if required.

When the examination is complete the telescope is removed, air allowed to escape and then the sheath removed. In ascites the peritoneal wound should be repaired, and in all patients the skin is closed with interrupted silk sutures.

The pulse and blood pressure are recorded at frequent intervals for 2–3 h, and the patient kept in hospital overnight before discharge.

Complications occur in about 1–2% of examinations, with an overall mortality of 0.03%. These deaths probably relate to liver biopsy, and the mortality is much lower than laparotomy. Problems which can arise include haemorrhage, bowel puncture, air embolism and puncture of an ovarian cyst.

Interpretation

The *cirrhotic* liver is nodular and in *hepatitis* the liver is red, swollen and shiny. A green liver is seen in *cholestatic* jaundice and various characteristics such as the state of the gallbladder and the liver edge have been claimed to help in the distinction between intra- and extrahepatic obstructive jaundice. Both primary and secondary *malignant disease of the liver* can be recognised. A *hepatoma* is often seen against the background of a cirrhotic liver and metastatic nodules are usually yellow-white and umbilicated. *Hydatid cysts* appear as characteristic pearly-white bulges.

Hydrops and fibrosis of the gallbladder can be identified.

The peritoneum is dull and opaque in the presence of ascites. In acute *tuberculous peritonitis* it may be possible to see multiple millet seed-sized nodules surrounded by a halo of congestion. This appearance is very similar to that of metastatic malignant disease involving the peritoneum and the differentiation is usually made by biopsy and histological examination of a nodule. In *chronic tuberculous peritonitis* there are extensive adhesions, the nodules are confluent and the mesentery is contracted.

Indications

(1) *Liver disease*

The inspection of the liver and targeted biopsy provides useful proof of diagnosis in alcoholic liver disease, macronodular as well as micronodular cirrhosis, hepatoma and metastatic carcinoma. Congenital cysts are usually readily recognised. Liver biopsy either by separate skin puncture or through the laparoscope can be used in patients with coagulation defects, because undue bleeding may be seen and controlled.

(2) *Acute abdomen*

In preliminary evaluation, especially suspected appendicitis, laparoscopy may avoid some unnecessary operations. This is particularly true in women of the childbearing years.

(3) *Ascites*

Liver disease, peritoneal carcinoma or tuberculosis can usually be readily identified as causes. A forceps biopsy is practicable for the peritoneum but should be avoided for the bowel.

(4) *Portal hypertension*

Dilated veins and splenic enlargement are seen.

(5) *Identification of masses*

Enlarged upper abdominal organs can usually be seen satisfactorily. Pelvic masses may also be seen and biopsied, but other abdominal masses are often obscured by bowel or omentum.

(6) *Others*

Laparoscopy can be combined with cholangiography by either hepatic or gallbladder puncture and in this way assists in the diagnosis of *jaundice*. It is probably inferior to laparotomy or CT scanning in the staging of *lymphoma*, but can be used as a preliminary procedure in patients with serious abdominal complaints not fully explained by full medication investigation.

The procedure is unsatisfactory in marked obesity and after major abdominal surgery or peritonitis. It must be performed with caution when there are coagulation defects. Removal of fluid is required with tense ascites and hypovolaemic collapse and encephalopathy are hazards together with persistent leakage.

LAPAROTOMY

The use of exploratory laparotomy has rightly decreased. Occasionally it still has a role in undiagnosed abdominal pain and in undiagnosed fever. In addition, a full review of abdominal contents may supplement or alter diagnoses made prior to planned surgery.

Further Reading

Bateson MC and Bouchier IAD. *Clinical Investigations in Gastroenterology*. Lancaster: Kluwer Academic Publishers, 1997

Cotton PB and Williams CB. *Practical Gastrointestinal Endoscopy*. Oxford: Blackwell Scientific Publications, 1996

Drossman DA. *Manual of Gastroenterologic Procedures*. New York: Raven Press, 1993

Haubrich WS, Schaffner F and Berk JE. *Bockus Gastroenterology*. Philadelphia: W.B. Saunders, 1995

McIntyre N, Benhamou JP, Bircher J, Rizzeto M and Rodes J. *Oxford Textbook of Clinical Hepatology*. Oxford: Oxford University Press, 1999

Sleisenger MH and Fordtran JS. *Gastrointestinal and Liver Disease*. Philadelphia: W.B. Saunders, 1998

Appendix
Common Diseases and Tests to Perform

Achalasia	Isotope swallow, barium swallow, endoscopy, chest X-ray
Acute intermittent porphyria	Urinary creatinine : porphyrin ratio
Acute pancreatitis	Serum amylase, abdominal US, abdominal CT, ERCP
Acute viral hepatitis	LFTs, IgM anti-HAV, HbsAg, anti-HCV
Alactasia	Milk challenge, hydrogen breath test after lactose
Alcoholic liver disease	LFTs, FBC, abdominal US, liver biopsy, chest X-ray
Alimentary hypoglycaemia	Glucose tolerance test with 10-min blood samples
α_1-Antitrypsin deficiency	Serum α_1-antitrypsin, phenotyping
Amoebiasis	Fresh stool hanging drop microscopy, serology
Amyloidosis	Rectal or liver biopsy
Angiodysplasia	Gastroscopy or colonoscopy
Appendicitis	Laparoscopy in women of childbearing years
Ascites	LFTs, diagnostic paracentesis, serum α-fetoprotein
Barrett's oesophagus	Gastroscopy, biopsy
Candida of oesophagus	Gastroscopy, biopsy
Carcinoid	Urine 5-hydroxyindoleacetic acid

147

Carcinoma gallbladder	Abdominal US, oral cholecystogram, laparoscopy
Carcinoma large bowel	Sigmoidoscopy, colonoscopy, biopsy, double-contrast barium enema
Carcinoma rectum	Digital examination, proctoscopy, biopsy
Cathartic colon	Sigmoidoscopy
Cholangiocarcinoma	ERCP, CT scan
Chronic autoimmune hepatitis	LFTs, immune globulins; nuclear, smooth muscle, LKM antibodies
Chronic pancreatitis	Abdominal X-ray, US, CT scan, ERCP, fasting and post-prandial plasma glucose
Chronic viral hepatitis	LFTs, HBsAg, HBeAg, anti-HCV, HBV DNA, HCV RNA
Cirrhosis	Liver biopsy, LFTs, abdominal US, HBsAg, anti-HCV, ferritin, α_1-antitrypsin; nuclear, smooth muscle, LKM, mitochondrial antibodies; serum copper
Coeliac disease	Endomysial antibody, small bowel biopsy
Colonic polyps	Colonoscopy or sigmoidoscopy with polypectomy or biopsy, barium enema
Colonic strictures	Colonoscopy, barium enema
Common bile duct stone	LFTs, abdominal US, ERCP, CT, MRCP
Crohn's disease	Small bowel meal, white blood cell scan, colonoscopy with biopsy, barium enema
Cutaneous porphyria	Urinary porphyrins
Cystic fibrosis	Gene testing, sweat test, pancreolauryl test
Diverticular disease	Barium enema
Drug hepatitis	LFTs, liver biopsy
Duodenal erosion	Gastroscopy
Duodenal ulcer	Gastroscopy, barium meal
Duodenitis	Gastroscopy
Dysentery	Stool culture, serology for amoeba and salmonella, blood culture
Food intolerance	Exclusion diet, IgE RAST, skin prick testing

Gallbladder stones	US, oral cholecystogram
Gastric carcinoma	Gastroscopy and biopsy, CT scan, LFTs, barium meal
Gastric erosions	Gastroscopy
Gastric lymphoma (MALToma)	Gastroscopy and biopsy
Gastric ulcer	Gastroscopy and biopsy, barium meal
Gastrinoma	Serum gastrin, basal/peak acid output
Gastritis	Gastroscopy
Gastro-oesophageal reflux	Gastroscopy, 24-h oesophageal pH, isotope swallow and reflux test
Gilbert's syndrome	Fractionated serum bilirubin, 48-h fast
Haematemesis	Gastroscopy, barium meal
Haemochromatosis	Serum ferritin, HFE gene testing, liver biopsy
Hepatitis A	IgM anti-HAV
Hepatitis B	HBsAg, HBeAg, HBV DNA
Hepatitis C	Anti-HCV, HCV RNA
Hiatus hernia	Gastroscopy, barium meal
Hirschsprung's disease	Barium enema, deep anorectal biopsy
Insulinoma	48-h fast with plasma glucose levels, glucose/insulin tolerance test
Ischaemic colitis	Barium enema, colonoscopy, angiography
Liver metastases	LFTs, US, CT, MRI, liver biopsy
Lymphangiectasia	Small bowel biopsy
Lymphoma	Small bowel biopsy, enteroscopy, small bowel meal
Mallor–Weiss tears	Gastroscopy
Melaena	Gastroscopy, colonoscopy, barium enema, angiography, red cell isotope scanning
Obscure chronic diarrhoea	Gastrin, vasoactive intestinal peptide, TSH, plasma glucose, HIV testing, triolein breath test

Obstructive jaundice	US, ERCP, CT
Oesophageal carcinoma	Gastroscopy and biopsy, barium swallow, CT, MRI
Oesophageal dysmotility	Isotope swallow, oesophageal manometry
Oesophageal stricture	Gastroscopy and biopsy, barium swallow
Oesophageal varices	Gastroscopy
Oesophagitis	Gastroscopy
Pancreatic carcinoma	LFTs, US, CT, MRI, ERCP, CA19-9
Partial gastrectomy sequelae	Gastroscopy, augmented glucose tolerance test, serum calcium, gastrin
Perforated abdominal viscus	Erect and supine plain radiograph
Peritonitis	Paracentesis, laparotomy
Phaeochromocytoma	Urinary catecholamines
Pharyngeal pouch	Barium swallow
Piles	Proctoscopy
Polyposis of colon	Sigmoidoscopy, barium enema
Portal gastropathy	Gastroscopy
Primary biliary cirrhosis	LFTs, mitochondrial and M_2 fraction antibody, liver biopsy
Primary liver cell carcinoma	US, CT, liver biopsy, α-fetoprotein
Primary sclerosing cholangitis	Liver biopsy, ERCP, anti-neutrophil cytoplasmic antibody (ANCA)
Pseudo-membranous colitis	Sigmoidoscopy, stool *Clostridium* enterotoxin, stool culture
Scleroderma	Gastroscopy; barium swallow, meal, follow-through
Ulcerative colitis	Sigmoidoscopy with biopsy, barium enema, colonoscopy
Whipple's disease	Small bowel biopsy
Wilson's disease	Liver biopsy, serum copper

Index

abscesses, 100, 121, 124
achalasia, 11, 16
achlorhydria, 20
acute appendicitis, 64
acute cholecystitis, 134, 135
acute intermittent porphyria, 111
acute peritoneal infections, 138
adenomatous polyps, 56, 59
adenomyomatosis, 130
alcoholic liver disease, 100, 104, 113,
    117, 119, 126, 143
alcoholism, 103
alimentary hyperglycaemia, 36
allergic symptoms, 102
amoebiasis, 63, 67, 68, 78
amoebic dysentery, 56
amoeboma, 63
ampulla of Vater, 4
ampullary strictures, 122
amyloid, 117
amyloidosis, 41, 59, 100
angiodysplasia, 43, 67, 75
angiography, 42
antibodies, gastric, 22
antibodies, intrinsic factor, 22
antibodies, parietal cell, 22
α_1-antitrypsin deficiency, 101, 102
appendicitis, acute, 64

bacterial dysentery, 56
bacterial overgrowth of the gut, 22
Barrett's oesophagus, 2, 9
bile acid malabsorption, 35
bile duct carcinoma, 131
bile duct stones, 85, 122
biliary atresia, 135
biliary disease, 100
biliary strictures, 7, 133
blind loops, 41
breath hydrogen, 45

cancer, *see* carcinoma
candida, oesophageal, 125

carcinoma, 3, 16, 122
  bile duct, 131
  colonic, 59, 61, 105
  gallbladder, 127, 130, 133
  gastric, 20, 22
  head of the pancreas, 126
  hepatic duct, 133
  hepatocellular, 117, 121, 124
  large bowel, 53, 56, 68
  liver, 100
  metastatic 117, 143
  metastatic of liver, 99
  oesophageal, 2, 4
  pancreatic 7, 31, 83, 85, 88, 96, 105,
    122
  peritoneal, 143
  prostatic, 52, 64
  rectal, 52, 53, 64
carcinoma-in-situ, 23
carotenaemia, 97
cathartic colon, 63
choledochal cysts, 127
cholestasis, 7, 97, 98, 103, 118, 126, 133
cholesterolosis, 130
chronic pancreatic disease, 31
chylous ascites, 139
cirrhosis, 99, 100, 102, 103, 117, 118,
    119, 123, 124, 125, 143
cirrhotic liver, 142
coeliac disease, 4, 31, 39, 40, 41, 48, 102
colitis
  acute, 61
  amoebic, 59
  Crohn's, 63
  ischaemic, 61, 63
  ulcerative, 56, 58, 59, 62, 67, 68
common bile duct stones, 7, 122, 126
computed tomography, 26, 85, 133
congenital cysts, 143
Crohn's disease, 41, 42, 43, 46, 52, 57,
    59, 67, 68, 75
CT scanning, 11, 85, 133
cystic fibrosis, 31, 93, 94

151